THE GOOD
Cat Food Guide

Authors' Note

All the foods tested here are of the highest quality required of cat food. This is a guide to taste, and other useful information such as availability, packaging, etc. The cat foods in our reports have, where possible, been tested by several cats, and ratings given by experienced cat owners according to our Paws & Claws Scale. Where scores differed, we have taken an average; where scores differed dramatically we have re-tested. The ratings and comments are made by cat owners who know their cats well and understand their reactions, and are not to be relied upon as a substitute for medical or veterinary advice.

For more information about making your feline an Honourary Inspector and joining the Feline International Gourmet Society go to www.goodcatfoodguide.com

First published in Great Britain 2006

1 3 5 7 9 10 8 6 4 2

Text © Rosemary and Andrew Gasson 2006
Illustrations © Kevin Oxlade

Rosemary and Andrew Gasson have asserted their right to be identified as the authors of this work under the Copyright, Designs and Patents Act 1988.

Ebury Press, an imprint of Ebury Publishing.
Random House, 20 Vauxhall Bridge Road, London SW1V 2SA

Random House Australia (Pty) Limited
20 Alfred Street, Milsons Point, Sydney, New South Wales 2061, Australia

Random House New Zealand Limited
18 Poland Road, Glenfield, Auckland 10, New Zealand

Random House (Pty) Limited
Isle of Houghton, Corner of Boundary Road and Carse O'Gowrie, Houghton, 2198, South Africa

Random House Publishers India Private Limited
301 World Trade Tower, Hotel Intercontinental Grand Complex, Barakhamba Lane, New Delhi 110 001, India

The Random House Group Limited Reg. No. 954009

www.randomhouse.co.uk

A CIP catalogue record for this book is available from the British Library.

Cover design by Nadine Bindeman/2 Associates
Typeset by Perfect Bound Ltd

ISBN 9780091910167 (after Jan 2007)
ISBN 0091910161

Papers used by Ebury Press are natural, recyclable products made from wood grown in sustainable forests.

Printed and bound in Singapore by Tien Wah Press

Acknowledgements

FELINE FOOD PURVEYORS
Arden Grange
Burgess Supafeeds
Butcher's Pet Care
Co-operative Group (CWS)
Denes Natural Pet Food
Healthy Options Pet Food
Marks & Spencer
Morrisons
Procter & Gamble
Royal Canin
Town & Country Petfoods
Trophy Pet Foods
Wafcol

TEMPORARY INSPECTORS
Smudge from Cricklewood
Spencer from Gerrards Cross

OTHERS
The Dragon Veterinary Clinic
Food Standards Agency
PFMA
The originator of any quotation we
might have ruined!

INTERMOG COUNSELLORS
Sonia Bramble
Alison Cockcroft
Richard Coote
Gail Eason
Alison Florence
Nicole Harrison

Gail Jones
Chris MacGuire
Edward Oxlade
Robert Oxlade
Arthur Payn
Ken Stirt
Becky White

CAT-FLAP CATERERS
Marie Amor
Perry Gard
Julie Laurie
Sarah Mindel
Kath Oxlade
Ginette Petrushkin
Karen Roston
Chrissie and Mickey Warren

FELINE RIGHTS LAWYER
Gillian Benning

THANK YOU!

The Inspectors

Dedicated to the memory of Bronte

CONTENTS

A Few Words of Introduction

from Waldo, the Chief Inspector, and the Editors

The world of feline eating has changed significantly since the guide was first published in 1992. Now, as then, the choice of cat food is enormous and still growing. In the 21st century, however, the internet and modern technology have opened up new avenues of exploration for discerning felines and their owners to seek out interesting and different foods.

We have fifteen full-time inspectors, representing a mixture of ages, breeds and sexes. We may have used some licence for their descriptions and unusual occupations, but they are all felines who have dedicated their limited waking hours to consuming vast quantities of the good, the bad and the not-very-good-looking cat food without any thought for their own welfare. However, the guide has its own Health & Safety Officer, Bennett Jr, to ensure no harm comes to any of them.

The team are all subject to continued recertification and training and must rigorously adhere to the guide's Code of Practice. They have learnt to be as objective and unbiased as the field allows. All keep in touch with head office by mobile phone and submit their reports by email on a weekly basis. Failure to comply invokes immediate suspension and loss of bonus treats.

Our research found an abundance of new brands, ranges and flavours. There are now many healthy-eating options as well as foods for specific medical conditions. We were delighted that some of the major manufacturers and supermarkets were willing to assist us in our research. Our aims are the same: to promote good, balanced, adventurous and, most importantly, healthy eating for felines.

We randomly allocate to each inspector a representative selection of foods from both large, well-known manufacturers and the smaller producers. Each product is tested individually and then rated on our Paws & Claws Scale from 0 to 5. Special note is made for cat foods of gastronomic excellence and crossed whiskers may be awarded for those of interest as 'Recommended eating'. At least three inspectors test each food and in the event of any disagreement the Chief Inspector adjudicates.

This guide remains independent in its editorial selection and does not accept advertising, payment or samples from any cat-food manufacturers. Real cats have genuinely tested all the cat foods mentioned in this guide. All the information was correct at the time of testing for brand name, flavour, pack size, etc., and taken from the labels or available manufacturers' fact sheets.

Since the first guide, most of our original inspectors have inevitably gone to the great cat basket in the sky, but we salute their pioneering years of dedicated service to feline eating. Although the guide currently has a full complement of enthusiastic inspectors, our Department of Feline Resources will soon be starting a new recruitment drive. During our research for this edition, alas, we lost Ziggy to a fatal case of stroke, and Snooks, who retired to Florida as he preferred a warmer climate and a seafood diet.

For this edition of *The Good Cat Food Guide*, we have changed some sections and added new ones. We hope that the following pages will give all our feline readers a flavour of both the traditional and new foods currently available, as well as offering guidance to their human owners.

Meanwhile, our investigations continue...

INTRODUCING OUR INSPECTORS
Arnie

My name is Arnie and I'm the team's computer expert and cybercat. I don't mind if they call me CTRL+EAT+DELETE (my favourite phrase) but I draw the line at office assistant. I'm much more important than that because I mastermind all the technology and emails. Without purring my own trumpet too much, it's all rather well done with digicat technology, using the control panel to keep them up to scratch and Microcat 2000™ for the food reports. Each inspector files reports in the My Food folder and with training they have all become efficient mouse users.

When tasting a newly discovered recipe, they now read the labels carefully to check the properties and enter them using the Food Wizard. If in doubt, they defer to Bennett Jr for health advice. I sometimes find it hard to convince them that a word processor is just as useful as a food processor – but at least they now understand that the toolbar is not used for opening tins of cat food.

I never go out as I'm rather agoraphobic but this doesn't matter because there's always Windows Explorer to view the world. I don't mind being on email duty 24 hours a day, so I've also set up a dedicated Inspectors' Helpline.

They just dial **0800 CATFOOD**, enter their pussword and then:

Press **1** to add or remove a cat food.

Press **2** to report a new brand or flavour.

Press **3** to recommend a food for an award.

Press **4** to purr.

Paw any key to continue…

Favourite Food: Gourmet Gold – Chicken & Liver in Gravy

Unusual Eating: Rich Tea biscuits, Hula Hoops

Hobbies: Keyboard sleeping and mouse to mouth

Favourite Quotation: 'Cats everywhere love Windows' (*Bill Gates*)

Bennett Jr

My name is Bennett Jr and I'm the guide's Health & Safety Officer. That's why my colleagues nicknamed me Hard Hat for short. I'm the son of Bennett from the original 1990s guide. He has now retired from official eating responsibilities but there's still a lot to be learned from his wise old taste buds.

I was originally trained as a Feline Rights lawyer. I've had many famous clients and handled Humphrey's compensation and re-housing claim for eviction from No. 10. I also help asylum-seeking felines, and you'll remember how I won the appeal to stop a three-legged Abyssinian single parent and her kittens being deported from Catwick.

When not food testing or practising feline law, I'm usually found writing policy manuals. *Safety in the Eating Place*, *The Control of Hazardous Cat Foods* and *The European Directive on the Prevention of Feline Accidents* are all my work. I also carry out the inspectors' training and make spot checks to ensure their adherence to *The Good Cat Food Guide Code of Practice* (2006, revised).

Additionally, my responsibilities include making sure the team wear their protective equipment when investigating new or unknown foods, such as scratchproof eating goggles to protect cats' eyes from exploding food pouches and whisker covers to avoid cross-contamination. I would also like a 'Slippery Floor' warning by every cat bowl to protect felines from clumsy humans.

I'd like to go down in history as a feline who has made a significant contribution to the safety of 21st-century cat food. My ambition is to follow in my father's footsteps and become President of FIGS – The Feline International Gourmet Society.

Favourite Food: Waitrose Special Recipe – Red Mullet & Tuna Chunks in Jelly

Unusual Eating: Unavailable – Data Protection Act

Hobbies: No time for hobbies – too many forms to fill in

Favourite Quotation: 'Our mission is to protect feline health and safety by ensuring risks in the changing eating place are properly controlled' (*Health & Safety Executive website, 2006*)

Bronte

My name is Bronte. I'm nearly fourteen and jet black in colour with just a few grey hairs. Apart from being Waldo's deputy when he goes AWOL, sometimes the team needs a steadying paw in the right direction, which only comes with age and maturity.

With a name like mine, I naturally became the literary member of the team. I don't go out much any more due to my advanced years and have plenty of time to read and shred books. There's so much to encourage felines in the world of literature. My favourite writer is Jane Austen – she wrote *Purrsuasion* – although I quite liked *Cat on a Hot Tin Roof*. There is also Edgar Allan Poe's *The Black Cat* and wasn't it Sherlock Holmes who coined the immortal phrase, 'Alimentary, my dear Watson'?

I can just about cope with the mobile phone – after all, there was a very good play entitled *An Inspector Calls*. I don't like to text because it wrecks the English language as well as my claws, so I have special permission from the chief to submit all my reports in writing.

Alas, due to ill health and an addiction to prescription drugs, my hobbies have become severely curtailed as the years have

progressed. However, I still indulge in bowl watching and give the occasional lecture to educate the younger felines on the evils of catnip addiction.

Favourite Food: HiLife Perfection – Steamed Hake with Tuna

Unusual Eating: Smoked salmon, salami sausage

Hobbies: Throwing up and sleeping (in no particular order)

Favourite Quotation: 'The only way to get rid of temptation is to yield to it' (*Oscar Wilde*)

The Camden Five

I'm Bibi the matriarch and I run the Camden Five gang with a paw of iron. A long time ago, I actually met the infamous arch villain, Macavity. I learned a lot from him, including how to be a master criminal. We had a lot of pressure from the other inspectors as they didn't want low-lifes like us in the book. So we had to make them an offer they couldn't refuse and now we are the official 'dry food' team.

Toozie is our enforcer and protects our territory from any feline upstart who attempts to take it over. He also does a nice line in counterfeit mice. He's originally from the Far East – a Siamese tabby or some such mixture – and when he forgot his feline passport once, he had to spend six months behind bars before they'd let him into the country. We had to call in a few favours from Bennett Jr and his Feline Rights contacts.

FB is my first lieutenant and is getting to be the brains of the outfit. He looks a bit like his brother Toozie, with that oriental look, but does have a slightly vicious streak, especially when it comes to birds or if teased by humans. However, he's very generous and

WANTED

TOOZIE   MIMI

BIBI

FB   BOYSIE

THE CAMDEN 5

always brings home the remains to leave in the kitchen. He is also very brave and once had to see off an urban fox.

Mimi is the good-looking one, the original glamour puss, although like all of us she knows where the fish bones are buried. She's a good girl but she really has this thing about fish – especially goldfish (very bling bling) – and leaves them all over the carpet if not eating them or wearing them as dangly earrings. She's very fashion-conscious and has the largest selection of designer cat collars you could ever imagine, ranging from Purbury to Mew Mew.

And finally there's Boysie. He's easy to describe: four legs, stripy black fur and, guess what, he's a cat burglar who knows all the best places to dine out or pinch food. Once he disappeared for a whole week. We thought he'd gone on witness protection but it turned out he'd just got locked in down the road. He really is a big softie and wouldn't harm a fly – unless he caught it!

Favourite Food: One Cat Adult – Chicken & Rice

Unusual Eating: Ice cream, cheese triangles

Hobbies: Breaking and entering, extortion

Favourite Quotation: 'Dogs come when they are called. Cats take a message and get back to you' (*Mary Bly*)

Jack

My nickname is JJ – Jack Junior – as I am the youngest member of the team. I'm eighteen months old, with a mainly black coat and white splodges around both my feet and nose (who said if your feet smell and your nose runs you were born upside-down?). Modesty precludes my mentioning that yellow eyes, a large square jaw and an immensely long tongue are my other feline attributes.

I was born in the heart of Essexland, and suppose that makes me a 'chav' cat. I'm always a bit wary when meeting new humans, but once I get to know them I enjoy nothing more than driving them crazy, playing 'tread the food into the carpet', 'knock the bowl over' or just shredding the daily newspaper. I'm also the inspectors' expert on mobile phones and IPAWS. Apart from Bronte, I've taught them all how to text.

But what I really enjoy is travel. I started with local trips to the other side of town to get the family used to my disappearing for two or three days at a time. Once I'd finished my GCSEat levels and found out about feline travel requirements, I got my microchip and passport from the vet and was off on my gap year. So far I've only been to northern Europe across the Channel, but with my Paw Miles I hope to go to the Canaries and Sardinia, as they sound like good eating places.

Favourite Food: Whiskas – Turkey in Gravy
Unusual Eating: Strawberry yoghurt
Hobbies: Chewing through cordless-telephone wires
Favourite Quotation: 'Normal people make good pets' (*Anon*)

Livingstone

My name is Livingstone but most cats call me Ken. I was named after a town in Scotland, although I now live in Catford. My fur is neatly trimmed and very ginger. Once I did try to change it by going green, but the result was a disaster as no one recognised me.

I take my duties as an inspector very seriously and organise assembly meetings for every report. These are always completed in red ink and I tell the team exactly how to vote. Despite rumours to the contrary, I keep telling the other felines that I am not plotting to oust the Chief Inspector and there are no plans to levy a digestion charge on eating at peak times. I am far too busy selling purrmits for every conceivable occasion and charging felines for arranging the Catolympics in 2012.

I hate motor cars and love to immobilise them by tyre scratching, and I'll do anything to make the roads safer for us felines. There is nothing nicer than lazing around in the sun on speed bumps without being disturbed by 4 x Paws. I decided that we have to treat humans like parking meters. We'll let them keep feeding us and when we've had enough it's time's up. If they want to show us off to their friends, they'll have to 'pay and display'. For hobbies, I love newt watching. I'm also a great art lover, especially the paintings of Bridget Riley, who paints the double yellow lines and boxes everywhere.

My favourite food used to be GaLA until they discontinued it. However, if I'm watching the budget, I always remember the advantages of Sainsbury's Supreme Cuts.

Favourite Food: Almo Nature – Tuna & Cheese

Unusual Eating: Hummus and sheeps' eyes

Hobbies: Newt watching

Favourite Quotation: 'If voting changed anything, they'd abolish it' (*Mayor of London,* 1987)

Ninja

M y name sounds rather aggressive and I like to strut around in a Ninja uniform, including my High Top Tabbi boots, pretending to be a black-belt martial arts expert. I hate to admit it but I'm really just a big wuss.

HiiiYAH!

I absolutely hate violence and exercise in that order. In fact, I think anything energetic should carry a government health warning: 'Exercise can seriously damage your health.' The only plank I ever broke was a second-hand cat flap. So instead of all that violent martial arts stuff, I practise tai chi and I'm currently learning pilates.

I'm five years old and rather prone to being overweight as I love to eat anything and everything that swims or moves slowly enough for me to catch, and prefer to sit quietly purring over my tuna and jelly.

Livingstone sometimes gives me a hard time when I go after his newts. He regards them more as friends than the lunch menu. However, the foods I really adore are mock turtle and chocolate turtle brownies.

Favourite Food: Nutro Natural Choice Weight Management – Chicken & Liver in Gravy

Unusual Eating: Human tuna, crisps and hamburgers (without the bun)

Hobbies: Meditating

Favourite Quotation: 'A cat food of a thousand mouthfuls begins with a single bite' (*Confucius,* 501 BC)

Poppy

My name's Poppy and I'm the gardening and undercover bird-watching expert on the team. I love the outdoors and usually spend most of my waking hours in the garden, studying the flora and fauna or trying to catch lunch if I'm wearing my twitcher's hat. I sometimes don my jungle camouflage and hide in the trees or bushes ready to pounce on some unsuspecting bird so that Shoes can create one of her Bird's Nest specials. Usually I send any fresh catch of the day direct to her cat flap by Intermog Couriers.

If the hunting isn't good I put on my red wellingtons and start digging up the neighbour's garden, where I've made a study of watching the catnip grass grow. I also cultivate catmint (*Nepeta faassenii* to us horticulturalists), which I often give to the other inspectors if they get bad breath.

I am currently trying to grow some new strains of cat grass, including camphor, Greek and lemon, and they tell me my pussy willow is the best in town.

I have to be careful when and where I sell my 'special' herbs as the catnip police are cracking down on illicit dealing and are giving Catsbos to my wilder friends.

If the weather's bad, I laze around indoors and watch one of my two favourite TV programmes: Charlie Dimmock on gardening or Bill Oddie on twitching. I also have to keep my birding book up to date and enter any new lunch delicacies.

Favourite Food: Felix Twice as Nice – Chicken, Turkey & Vegetables

Unusual Eating: Fish and chips, cheese and onion crisps

Hobbies: Sitting on newspapers and magazines and leaving dirty paw prints

Favourite Quotation: 'The early bird may get the worm, but the second mouse gets the cheese' (*Anon*)

Shoes

My name is Shoes. I'm nine years old, and petite with slim hips, delicate features and brown tabby markings. I recently had highlights put into my fur to give me more feline appeal. Being single, I would like to meet a handsome tom who can give me a few wild nights on the tiles.

I think I must have been Nefertiti in a previous incarnation because, like my friend Delia, I am a domestic goddess – feline variety. Cooking and creating interesting recipes for felines are what I live and purr for.

Most days I'm to be found in the kitchen whipping up some

of my favourite dishes for the other inspectors when they're off duty. My friend Meow-Meow helps me lick out the bowls when I'm finished – anything to save washing up.

I hope one day that the cat-food manufacturers will take a leaf out of my recipe book and produce such delicacies as Devilled Dogs, Persian Chicken and Sautéed Catfish with Ginger Tom Sauce. I also enjoy creating the desserts that follow. My favourite is Bird's Nest Pudding, depending on the seasonal catch of the day, which Poppy sends over by Intermog Couriers.

My idols from the world of cooking include such masters of the crossed whisker as Two Fat Felines, Rick Strine the Australian and of course Nigella Pawson. Ultimately I would like to run my own restaurant called Chez Moggie.

Favourite Food: Waitrose Special Recipe – Rabbit & Game

Unusual Eating: Ice cream, roast beef

Hobbies: Carpet shredding and sleeping

Favourite Quotation: 'Too many cooks spoil the cat food' (*Anon*)

Sox

I'm a ten-year-old tortoiseshell with dashes of white around my face and I live in a large oak-panelled house in the posh part of Middlesex. The advantage of this is the super-sized garden, which gives me space to carry out all my sporting activities.

I adore games of all sorts, especially table tennis. Ping-pong balls are just the right size to kick around or chew and I love the noise they make.

What I really like are extreme sports. I work on the principle that if I've got nine lives then I should use them all. Indoors, the best is curtain abseiling but it only works when my claws are really sharp. I also go in for wall-of-death bathtub racing.

Outdoors, I try either window-ledge jumping or washing-line walking – anything high-wire to get the adrenaline pumping and worry the humans. I love it when they call the fire brigade. But what really annoys them is the last-second dash to the favourite armchair before they close the back door.

Sometimes, I prefer just to watch TV sports like snooker where I can follow the ball across the screen with my paw. But that's only practice for football. I love to watch my favourite team, Norwich City, and catch those canaries on the screen.

Favourite Food: Go-Cat Vitality+ – Turkey & Green Beans

Unusual Eating: Human chicken, chicken soup

Hobbies: Dreaming of winning a gold medal in the 2012 Catolympics

Favourite Quotation: 'It is not the winning, it's the taking apart' (*Anon*)

Waldo (The Chief Inspector)

I'm Waldo, Chief Inspector of *The Good Cat Food Guide*. At two years old I'm a rather impressive specimen of Maine Coon tabby with a pedigree as long as your proverbial paw. My parents were international champions and I am told that I have a physique to die for. However, I'm an unassuming sort of feline and usually pretend to be just an ordinary moggie from a battered felines' refuge in Streatham.

I'm almost 18lbs in weight, with very big hairy ears, extremely large feet and a long shaggy fur coat that keeps me warm in winter and is drip-dry and self-grooming. It also makes a bold fashion statement along with my dark glasses and ring-pull earring. My proudest attribute is a 16-inch-long fluffy tail, which looks like a flagpole most of the time.

Because of my size I need to eat a lot, a sensible prerequisite of the job, and it makes me well qualified for the role of Chief Inspector. Some of the older and more experienced members of the team were rather disconcerted at my appointment but I put that down to the green-eyed monster. I know where the fish bones are buried and got the job anyway!

I was recently microchipped for security and I'm now linked into a CatNav GPS. This way my personal bodyguard can always locate me and protect me from catnapping.

Apart from eating, my favourite occupation is breaking things, although my human thinks I'm just accident prone. Either way, I must own up to a long list of damage: one flat-screen television (my greatest disaster to date – lovely noise), assorted antiques, a new leather couch, three kitchen pedal bins and an electric kettle. I heard that's what pet insurance is for! Anyway, the family motto is 'Destroy with impunity'.

Favourite Food: Whiskas Organic Turkey & Veggies in Gravy

Unusual Eating: Elastic bands and yucca plants

Hobbies: Fishing from the garden pond and catching treats with my paws

Favourite Quotation: 'Paw, paw is better than claw, claw' (*Winston Churchill,* 1954)

Feline Fact File

'A fat cat is a happy cat but not a healthy cat'
(*The Good Cat Food Guide*, 1992)

Food Types

Wet foods

Wet foods are sold in tins, foil packs or pouches.

- Usually complete
- Available in a wide variety of flavours
- Practical
- Store well until open
- Tastier
- Nutritious
- May contain up to 85% moisture

Dry foods

Dry foods are sold in cartons, boxes or sacks.

- Usually complete
- Store well
- Give virtually no wastage
- More pleasant to handle for humans
- Minimum odour
- Usually contain less fat
- Typically contain 8–9% moisture
- May contain salt to encourage drinking

NB Fluids MUST be added to the diet.

There is a third type of food called semi-moist, which used to be widely available but eluded all of our research for this edition of the guide.

Complete foods

These contain all the nutrients necessary for a properly balanced feline diet. They usually include beneficial additives such as minerals and vitamins. The majority of cat foods are complete.

Complementary foods

These should only supplement complete foods. However tasty, they are not nutritionally balanced and long term will not ensure a healthy feline diet. Complementary foods include some special flavours and treats. Most cats enjoy human food but unless this is specially prepared with the necessary additives it does not contain all of the essential nutrients for a balanced feline diet.

Variety, High, Rich in, Flavour and With

These descriptions do not appear to have the strict legal definitions required for human food. Most manufacturers adopt the PFMA recommendations.

- A named ingredient (e.g. lamb) should be present as a minimum of 26%
- 'High' or 'rich in' (e.g. chicken) denotes a minimum of 14% 'flavour' or 'with' (e.g. tuna) requires a minimum of just 4%

Several foods from the same range could all consist of an identical main recipe. This explains why some fish varieties contain animal derivatives and vice versa. This 'core' recipe may vary from time to time (depending on the ingredients available) and could be the reason why perceptive felines suddenly go off their favourite food.

Labels

Bennett Jr thinks there are as many (if not more) regulations concerning pet food as human food. (The good news is that certain unmentionable body parts are prohibited, as are whales and dolphins.)

The label must include details of composition, moisture content for wet foods, added vitamins, minerals, preservatives and colouring, and manufacturing and sell-by dates. Pet-food manufacturers are very good at providing all of this information because (a) they are nice people and (b) they will be fined £5,000 if they don't.

The Average Feline...

- Weighs 7–12lbs (3.5–5.5kg). A good average is 9lbs (4kg) – but there are cats like Waldo, who weighs in at nearly 18lbs!

- Requires about 400 calories per day (equivalent very approximately to 350–400g of wet food or 70–90g of dry food – but this will depend on feline size, age and activity as well as the calorie content of the particular food). A large male should therefore eat up to about one large tin per day, three 100g pouches or 80g of dry food.

- Needs one large or two to three small meals per day of wet food or several small meals of dry food. A small female should eat up to two-thirds to three-quarters of the male's consumption.

- Junior felines (up to one year) need approximately double the energy per body weight compared with adults. There are several formulations of kitten food.

● Senior felines (over ten years) need three to six meals per day with a total consumption of about three-quarters of that of a younger feline. Adult formulations add ingredients such as glucosamine to help joints.

A Good Diet Must Contain...

● Animal protein (i.e. meat). Felines go under the fancy title of 'obligate carnivores'. Vegetable protein (e.g. soya) does not contain the necessary nutrients. There is, however, at least one variety of prepared vegan cat food which is nutritionally balanced with manufactured ingredients.

● On a moisture-free basis, 26–35% protein and 15–25% animal fat.

● A careful balance of at least thirteen vitamins.

● Vitamin A – most important for night vision, correct weight, good skin and fertility – but avoid it in excess.

● Taurine – the essential amino acid to prevent heart and eye problems.

● Fish oils, which contain Vitamin D3, essential for bone development – but avoid excess cod liver oil.

● Fluids, especially with dry foods. A loss of more than 10–15% of body fluids could be fatal. Some felines don't appear to drink; they may obtain sufficient fluid from wet foods but can't from dry foods.

Miscellaneous Diet Tips

- Dry foods are nutritionally more concentrated than wet foods so felines need smaller portions. The balance of ingredients also differs.

- Felines prefer food in lumps because of their teeth; they tear rather than chew. There are special foods now available for some breeds, such as Maine Coons, carefully prepared to suit the shape of their mouth (Waldo using his influence again).

- Pouch foods are usually less cooked than tinned foods and may taste more appealing. However, several are complementary.

- Fish is best steamed or baked to preserve the nutrients but be careful with bones.

- It is natural to eat grass to help regurgitate fur balls (but regular combing may prevent their formation). There are now 'hairball control' foods.

- Dry foods may help keep teeth free from tartar and there are special dental care diets – but again remember to give plenty of water.

- The chlorine in fresh tap water may irritate sensitive feline noses so 'stale' water may be preferred.

- Many vets advise against feeding cows' milk – some felines (including kittens) are physically unable to digest it and could end up with diarrhoea. There are now low-lactose varieties available.

- Catnip (catmint) is not addictive but according to Poppy it makes a feline very happy.

- Some foods include yucca extract, which in polite feline society is called a deodoriser.

- If your feline's stomach is touching the ground, he's a fat cat of the wrong sort. He might be able to buy a peerage but obesity could lead to serious health problems such as diabetes, so weigh him from time to time to make sure the avoirdupaws are under control. (The Camden Five call them natural born kilos.)

- If reducing the quantity in a fat feline's diet, try using a smaller bowl.

- If altering a feline's diet (e.g. from wet to dry food), make the change slowly, and check with the vet if in any doubt.

What To Avoid...

- Feeding baby food if your feline is feeling poorly. It may contain onion, which is toxic and could lead to anaemia.

- Old and rancid food – it can make felines ill and in any case they are far too sensible to eat it.

- Chilled food (e.g. straight from the fridge). Felines prefer lunch at room temperature or slightly warm, but heating to more than 110°F/43°C destroys food enzymes.

- Small bones in poultry or rabbit (they become more brittle with cooking). Fish bones, if well cooked till soft, can be safe and a good source of calcium.

- Too little water relative to dry food – it could cause urinary problems. Some specialist brands overcome this but if your feline is thought to have a problem it is better to feed wet foods and make water readily available.

- Too much liver – not more than 20% of a meal twice a week despite the addictive taste. Excess is dangerous because it causes problems with bones and joints.

- Too much lean meat (e.g. pure steak with no fat); it could lead to calcium, iodine and Vitamin A deficiencies unless these are supplied separately.

- Too many fish fillets (instead of meat) – they can cause vitamin deficiencies. Whole fish is fine.

- Raw fish – it must be cooked to remove unwanted enzymes which destroy essential nutrients. Only Japanese Ninja has a very occasional dispensation.

- Raw egg, except in very small quantities. It also neutralises other essential nutrients.

- Dog food (urrgh!) – it contains only about half the protein necessary for a good feline diet.

NOTE

We have found no evidence of the sometimes suggested notion that cat-food manufacturers put an addictive compound into their foods. The most important characteristic for most felines is smell. If they don't like the aroma then they won't eat it. Feline taste buds, on the other hand, are stimulated by additives like amino acids.

Guide to Symbols Used

Paws & Claws

= Outstanding – a gastronomic delight

= Good – delicious eating

= Quite good – tasty eating

= Very average – boring eating

🐾

= Below average – only eaten when desperate

No paws =

Refused to eat

In addition to the Paws & Claws rating, **Crossed Whiskers** are awarded to cat foods of outstanding gastronomic interest – 'Recommended eating'

Cat foods nominated for a **Golden Whiskers** award are marked with an asterisk *

Food Type

💧 Wet

☀️ Dry

Available from

🅢 Supermarket

🅟 Pet shop

🅐 Online

🅥 Vets

Packaging

🥫 Tin

Pouch

Pot

Sack

Box

Foil

FOOD REPORTS

Food Report No. 1
Almo Nature

Flavour:	Tuna & Cheese
Packaging:	🧴
Food Type:	💧
Manufacturer:	Almo Nature
Pack Size:	70g
Available From:	Ⓟ ⓐ
Inspector:	**Livingstone**
Paws & Claws Rating:	🐾 🐾 🐾 🐾 🐾

Notes:
One of several brands with unusual flavours purchased online, although now available in selected UK pet shops. 140g tins also available and a dry-food range called Almo Nature Holistic. All very expensive but the team loved them.

Supplementary Reports:
Atlantic Tuna Bronte 4, Jack 3, Ninja 3, Waldo 4
Chicken & Cheese Bennett Jr 5, Boysie 2, Jack 5, Mimi 0
Chicken & Pumpkin Bronte 0, Shoes 1, Waldo 1
Chicken & Shrimp Bennett Jr 1, Bibi 1, FB 1, Jack 4, Ninja 5
Salmon & Carrots Arnie 4, Poppy 5
Tuna & Corn Bibi 4, Boysie 4, FB 4, Mimi 4, Ninja 5, Toozie 5
White Fish Bennett Jr 4, Livingstone 4

Human Comments:

Remember when purchasing online, postage or courier charges must be added to the cost.

Inspector's Comment:
All I need now is the brown bread and the mayo.

Food Report No. 2
Almo Nature
Holistic Croquettes

Flavour:	Organic Chicken
Packaging:	
Food Type:	☀
Manufacturer:	Almo Nature
Pack Size:	400g
Available From:	Ⓟ ⓐ
Inspector:	**Camden Five**
Paws & Claws Rating:	🐾 🐾 🐾 🐾

Notes:
A range using only natural ingredients and entirely free of artificial additives, flavourings and preservatives. Manufactured in Italy; interesting but quite expensive.

Supplementary Reports:
Organic Chicken Bronte 2, Livingstone 3; *Salmon* Waldo 2

Inspector's Comment:
This bird can come home to roost any day...

Food Report No. 3
Animonda Rafiné Soupé

Flavour:	Chicken, Duck & Noodles
Packaging:	🥫
Food Type:	💧
Manufacturer:	Animonda
Pack Size:	100g
Available From:	Ⓟ ⓐ
Inspector:	**Bennett Jr**
Paws & Claws Rating:	🐾 🐾 🐾 🐾

Notes:
Other ranges include Animonda Carny Adult, Fish Menu, Rafiné Ragout and Soft Pâté. All have an exciting choice of flavour combinations, which gave the inspectors the chance to be adventurous but expensive eaters.

Supplementary Reports:
Carny Adult Mixed Meat Cocktail Shoes 4
Carny Adult Turkey & Rabbit Jack 0, Ninja 1
Fish Menu Sardine & Shrimp Bronte 5, Waldo 4
Fish Menu Seafood Platter Livingstone 5, Poppy 5
Fish Menu Tuna Ragout Arnie 5, Shoes 5
Rafiné Soft Pâté Beef & Heart Bennett Jr 2, Ninja 1
Rafiné Soupé Beef, Goose & Mortadella Arnie 5, Livingstone 2
Rafiné Soupé Poultry, Rabbit & Ham Jack 0, Sox 2
Rafiné Soupé Turkey, Veal & Cheese Bronte 2, Waldo 1

Inspector's Comment:
Tested to British Feline Eating Standard (BFES-2006) and passed with flying feathers.

Food Report No. 4
Arden Grange

Flavour:	Adult Chicken & Rice*
Packaging:	
Food Type:	
Manufacturer:	Leander International Pet Foods
Pack Size:	500g
Available From:	P 5 @ V
Inspector:	Sox
Paws & Claws Rating:	🐾 🐾 🐾 🐾

Notes:
Adult Salmon & Rice, Chicken & Rice, and Kitten Chicken & Rice complete the range. Also available in 2.5 and 7.5kg sacks. A good, simple, nutritionally balanced dry-food range.

Supplementary Reports:
Adult Chicken & Rice Bronte 4, Waldo 5; *Light Chicken & Rice* Jack 5, Ninja 3

Inspector's Comment:
This is not a chicken joke – this is the real thing!

Food Report No. 5

Arthur's Supermeat

Flavour:	Game & Liver
Packaging:	🥫
Food Type:	💧
Manufacturer:	Nestlé Purina Petcare
Pack Size:	400g
Available From:	Ⓟ Ⓢ ⓐ
Inspector:	**Jack**
Paws & Claws Rating:	🐾 🐾 🐾

Notes:
Several flavours available in this rather predictable range.

Supplementary Reports: *Beef & Chicken* Bibi 1, Boysie 4, FB 2, Mimi 1; *Chicken & Rabbit* Bennett Jr 1, Livingstone 5; *Chicken & Tuna* Boysie 4, Jack 0, Ninja 5, Poppy 1, Toozie 3, Waldo 5

Human Comments:
Well received by Jack because he was hungry.

Inspector's Comment:
This was fair game!

Food Report No. 6
Asda Tiger

Flavour:	Beef & Heart in Gravy
Packaging:	
Food Type:	
Manufacturer:	Asda
Pack Size:	100g
Available From:	⑤ (Asda)
Inspector:	**Ninja**
Paws & Claws Rating:	🐾 🐾 🐾

Notes:
An own-label brand with a wide choice of wet and dry foods for cats of all ages. There are ranges in sauces, jelly and gravy; available in single-serve pouches, foil trays and small and large tins. Asda also produce an economy range – for hard-up felines.

Supplementary Reports:
Chicken & Turkey in Gravy Bronte 4, Jack 1, Poppy 2, Shoes 3;
Chicken & Turkey in Jelly Arnie 4, Jack 1, Poppy 4, Waldo 3; *Lamb & Beef in Jelly* Jack 4, Sox 2;
Rabbit & Chicken in Jelly Bibi 2, Boysie 3, FB 2, Toozie 2; *Salmon & Chicken in Jelly* Jack 3, Livingstone 4, Mimi 1, Ninja 4

Inspector's Comment:
The way to a cat's heart is through its stomach…

Food Report No. 7
Asda Tiger

Flavour:	Duck, Rabbit & Vegetables
Packaging:	
Food Type:	
Manufacturer:	Asda
Pack Size:	375g
Available From:	⑤ (Asda)
Inspector:	**Shoes**
Paws & Claws Rating:	🐾 🐾 🐾

Notes:
Other flavours available in this
dry-food range include Chicken,
Turkey & Calcium, Duck, Rabbit
& Vegetables and a Kitten variety
of Chicken, Turkey & Milk.

Supplementary Reports: *Chicken,
Turkey & Calcium* Poppy 2;
*Kitten Chicken, Turkey &
Milk* Jack 4

**Inspector's
Comment:** *A
modest little cat
food with much
to be modest
about.*

Food Report No. 8

Asda Tiger Select Cuts

Flavour:	Tender Fillets of Turkey, Bacon & Chives
Packaging:	
Food Type:	
Manufacturer:	Asda
Pack Size:	100g
Available From:	Ⓢ (Asda)
Inspector:	**Waldo**
Paws & Claws Rating:	🐾 🐾 🐾

Notes:
Various flavours available.

Supplementary Reports:
Cod & Shrimp in Sauce
Jack 1, Ninja 2; *Mackerel
& Coley in Sauce* Bronte 0,
Jack 2; *Rabbit &
Chicken in Jelly*
Waldo 4

**Inspector's
Comment:**
*My idea of an
agreeable cat
food – a cat food
that agrees with
me!*

Food Report No. 9
Brekkies

Flavour:	Salmon, Trout & Pilchard
Packaging:	
Food Type:	
Manufacturer:	Affinity
Pack Size:	1kg
Available From:	Ⓟ Ⓢ @
Inspector:	Livingstone
Paws & Claws Rating:	🐾 🐾 🐾

Notes:
A long-established range, still well received and available in various flavours and sizes. Brekkies Excel Delice in several flavours and Excel Cat Rolls are two recent additions to the range. Another Affinity product is veterinary-formulated Ultima Adult – a complete dry cat food in Chicken & Rice.

Supplementary Reports:
Chicken & Turkey Bibi 4, Boysie 3, Bronte 4, Mimi 3
Rabbit, Chicken & Liver Bennett Jr 3, FB 3, Mimi 3, Toozie 3,
 Waldo 2

Inspector's Comment: *This was a bit middle-of-the-road!*

Food Report No. 10

Burgess Supa Cat

Flavour:	Rabbit & Chicken*
Packaging:	
Food Type:	
Manufacturer:	Burgess Supa Cat
Pack Size:	2kg
Available From:	Ⓟ Ⓢ ⓐ
Inspector:	**Camden Five**
Paws & Claws Rating:	🐾 🐾 🐾 🐾 🐾

Notes:
A complete dry-food range; also produced in Ocean Fish and
Chicken & Duck flavours, in various sizes.

Supplementary Reports:
Chicken & Duck Bronte 4, Waldo 4
Ocean Fish Bennett Jr 4, Livingstone 3

Human Comments:
*They couldn't get enough of this; even a 2kg sack divided by five
didn't last long.*

Inspector's Comment: *A star! This certainly has the X factor!*

Food Report No. 11
Classic

Flavour:	Beef Chunks in Jelly
Packaging:	
Food Type:	
Manufacturer:	Butcher's Pet Care
Pack Size:	100g
Available From:	(P) (S) (a)
Inspector:	**Bronte**
Paws & Claws Rating:	🐾 🐾 🐾

Notes:
100% natural flavoured and preservative free with no added
cereal or soya. Chicken, Game, Haddock, Ocean Fish and
several other flavours also available in single-serve 100g pouches
or 400g tins.

Supplementary Reports:
Chicken in Jelly Arnie 4, Boysie 4,
Sox 4, Toozie 3; *Game in Jelly**
FB 3, Livingstone 4, Shoes 4,
Waldo 4; *Rabbit & Chicken in
Jelly* Bennett Jr 3, Bronte 4,
Sox 4, Toozie 4, Waldo 5

Inspector's Comment:
*As they say in the classics, much
ado about nothing.*

Food Report No. 12
Classic

Flavour:	Haddock in Jelly
Packaging:	🥫
Food Type:	💧
Manufacturer:	Butcher's Pet Care
Pack Size:	400g
Available From:	Ⓟ Ⓢ ⓐ
Inspector:	**Bennett Jr**
Paws & Claws Rating:	🐾 🐾 🐾 🐾

Notes:
100% natural flavoured and preservative free. Several other flavours available.

Supplementary Reports:
Ocean Fish in Jelly Arnie 1, Bibi 3, FB 3, Mimi 3, Toozie 3; *Scottish Salmon in Jelly* Bronte 3, Waldo 5; *Trout in Jelly* Sox 4, Waldo 4

Inspector's Comment:
This sounded high on the purrometer!

Food Report No. 13

Co-op Complete Dry Cat Food

Flavour:	Chicken, Turkey & Milk
Packaging:	
Food Type:	
Manufacturer:	Co-operative Group (CWS)
Pack Size:	375g
Available From:	⑤ (Co-op)
Inspector:	**Camden Five**
Paws & Claws Rating:	🐾 🐾 🐾

Notes:
Available in several other flavours and 950g packs.

Supplementary Reports:
Rabbit, Duck & Vegetables Shoes 3, Livingstone 3

Inspector's Comment:
This was poultry by name – but not paltry by nature.

Food Report No. 14
Co-op Gourmet

Flavour:	Fine Terrine of Duck & Rabbit
Packaging:	
Food Type:	
Manufacturer:	Co-operative Group (CWS)
Pack Size:	100g
Available From:	⑤ (Co-op)
Inspector:	**Arnie**
Paws & Claws Rating:	🐾 🐾 🐾 🐾

Notes:
An own-label brand that includes Choice Chunks, Select Cuts
and Supreme; in either jelly or gravy, and
an economy range. Available in single-
serve pouches and tins.

Supplementary Reports:
Choice Chunks Tuna in Jelly
Bibi 2, FB 2, Jack 3; *Gourmet
Select Cuts Chicken, Ham &
Chives* Sox 3; *Gourmet Select
Cuts Salmon & Chicken in Jelly*
Livingstone 4

Human Comments:
*A good, well-thought-out brand at
reasonable prices.*

Inspector's Comment:
Love at first byte.

Co-op Supreme

Flavour:	Tuna in Jelly
Packaging:	🧴
Food Type:	💧
Manufacturer:	Co-operative Group (CWS)
Pack Size:	100g
Available From:	⑤ (Co-op)
Inspector:	**Poppy**
Paws & Claws Rating:	🐾 🐾 🐾 🐾

Notes:
The Co-op's Supreme range is available in both single-serve portions and 400g tins in either jelly or gravy.

Supplementary Reports:
Chicken in Jelly Shoes 2, Waldo 3; *Chicken & Turkey in Gravy* Boysie 3, FB 2, Jack 3, Mimi 2; *Tuna & Chicken Chunks in Jelly* Bennett Jr 3, Waldo 4; *Turkey & Liver in Gravy* Livingstone 3

Inspector's Comment:
Didn't mind going down the garden path for this one.

Food Report No. 16

Cuisine Chunks

Flavour:	Beef & Turkey in Gravy
Packaging:	
Food Type:	
Manufacturer:	Pets At Home
Pack Size:	100g
Available From:	℗ (Pets At Home)
Inspector:	**Shoes**
Paws & Claws Rating:	🐾 🐾 🐾

Notes:
Cuisine is Pets At Home's own-label range; vitamin enhanced. Pets At Home is a chain of pet superstores located all over the UK – worth a look.

Supplementary Reports:
Chicken & Lamb in Gravy Bronte 4, Waldo 3; *Trout in Jelly* Jack 1, Ninja 3

Inspector's Comment:
Mais oui – I love defenceless animals – especially in gravy!

Denes Adult – Original

Flavour:	Chicken & Turkey plus Added Herbs
Packaging:	🥫
Food Type:	💧
Manufacturer:	Denes Natural Pet Care
Pack Size:	400g
Available From:	Ⓟ Ⓢ ⓐ
Inspector:	Sox
Paws & Claws Rating:	🐾 🐾

Notes:

Three Denes ranges are free from artificial colourings and flavourings. The canned food covers Kitten, Adult and Gourmet in a wide selection of flavours plus added herbs. The single-serve range has several flavours in 100g foil trays. The complete dry foods include rice and added herbs in 500g and 2kg sizes.

Supplementary Reports:

Chicken & Turkey plus Added Herbs Shoes 3
Kitten Rabbit & Chicken plus Added Herbs Jack 2, Shoes 2
Rabbit & Chicken plus Added Herbs Bennett Jr 2, Livingstone 3
Salmon & Tuna plus Added Herbs Arnie 3
Turkey & Lamb plus Added Herbs Bronte 1, Shoes 2, Waldo 3

Inspector's Comment:
*Not worth killing two birds
with one stone for.*

Food Report No. 18
Eukanuba Adult Maintenance

Flavour:	Lamb & Liver
Packaging:	
Food Type:	
Manufacturer:	Iams
Pack Size:	2kg
Available From:	(P) (S) (a) (V)
Inspector:	**Waldo**
Paws & Claws Rating:	🐾 🐾 🐾 🐾

Notes:
Eukanuba produce a large selection of complete wet and
dry foods for kittens, adults and seniors. They include Light,
Maintenance, High Calorific and Hairball. Also available – but
only from vets – are both wet and dry Prescription Diets for
feline medical problems (kidneys, intestines, etc.).

Supplementary Reports:
Adult Light Chicken & Liver Livingstone 3
Intestinal Medical Diet (prescribed by Bronte's medical team)
   Bronte 5
Salmon & Rice Bennett Jr 4

Inspector's Comment: *I can't pronounce it but I like it.*

Food Report No. 19
Felix Roasted

Flavour:	Rabbit in Gravy
Packaging:	
Food Type:	
Manufacturer:	Nestlé Purina Petcare
Pack Size:	100g
Available From:	ⓟ ⓢ ⓐ
Inspector:	**Ninja**
Paws & Claws Rating:	🐾 🐾 🐾 🐾

Notes:
The Roasted range is a recent addition to the brand. Felix has several ranges in single-serve pouches, foil trays and tins in various sizes; a large choice of flavours in jelly and gravy with steaklets and pâté style also on offer. Quite new is a range of fish and meat foil trays with added vegetables. Felix is generally available for kittens, juniors, adults and seniors, and there is also a complete dry biscuit.

Supplementary Reports:
Beef, Duck & Peas in Jelly Bronte 4, Poppy 4, Sox 3, Waldo 3
Chicken, Liver & Carrots Livingstone 4
Haddock, Cod & Green Beans in Jelly Arnie 4, Bronte 4
Plaice, Salmon & Peas Bennett Jr 3, Shoes 4
Roasted Lamb Bronte 4, Waldo 5
Roasted Rabbit in Gravy Bennett Jr 4, Livingstone 4, Waldo 4

Inspector's Comment: *Another cat food – another miracle!*

Food Report No. 20
Felix

Flavour:	Cod & Plaice in Jelly
Packaging:	🥫
Food Type:	💧
Manufacturer:	Nestlé Purina Petcare
Pack Size:	400g
Available From:	Ⓟ Ⓢ ⓐ
Inspector:	**Bennett Jr**
Paws & Claws Rating:	🐾 🐾 🐾 🐾 🐾

Notes:
The Felix brand covers tins, pouches and foil trays (see Report 19). They also have a large pouch range, 'As Good As It Looks', with steaklets in various flavours.

Supplementary Reports:
Beef in Jelly Arnie 4, Bennett Jr 3, Livingstone 4, Shoes 3
Beef Supermeat with Lamb Bennett Jr 3, Livingstone 2
Chicken in Jelly Arnie 5, Ninja 5, Poppy 5, Shoes 3, Waldo 4
Duck & Heart in Jelly* Bennett Jr 5, FB 5, Sox 4, Toozie 5
Lamb Boysie 5, Mimi 4, Poppy 3, Toozie 5
Senior Beef in Jelly Arnie 4, Bronte 5
Senior Duck in Jelly Bennett Jr 4, Livingstone 5

Inspector's Comment: *I'd put my job on the line for this one!*

Food Report No. 21

Felix Complete

Flavour:	Complete Fish – Salmon, Tuna & Vegetables and Cereals
Packaging:	
Food Type:	
Manufacturer:	Nestlé Purina Petcare
Pack Size:	400g
Available From:	Ⓟ Ⓢ ⓐ
Inspector:	**Camden Five**
Paws & Claws Rating:	🐾 🐾 🐾 🐾 🐾

Notes:
Available in several flavours with 'tasty shapes'.

Supplementary Reports:
Chicken, Turkey & Vegetables Boysie 5, FB 4, Mimi 3, Toozie 4

Inspector's Comment:
Lead us not into temptation; just tell us where to steal it!

Food Report No. 22
Go-Cat Vitality+

Flavour:	Game, Turkey & Green Beans
Packaging:	
Food Type:	
Manufacturer:	Nestlé Purina Petcare
Pack Size:	100g
Available From:	P S a
Inspector:	**Arnie**
Paws & Claws Rating:	🐾 🐾 🐾 🐾

Notes:
A wide range of flavour combinations in either gravy or jelly; also available in 400g tins.

Supplementary Reports:
Chicken & Duck in Gravy Bennett Jr 4, Bronte 2, Poppy 4, Waldo 4; *Cod & Green Beans in Gravy* Livingstone 4, Sox 2; *Plaice & Carrots in Gravy* Arnie 5, Bennett Jr 5, Bronte 4, Sox 5; *Rabbit & Liver in Jelly* FB 4, Livingstone 5,

Inspector's Comment:
This definitely charged up the battery.

Food Report No. 23
Go-Cat Vitality+ Adult

Flavour:	Tuna, Herring & Vegetables*
Packaging:	🗋
Food Type:	☀
Manufacturer:	Nestlé Purina Petcare
Pack Size:	375g
Available From:	Ⓟ Ⓢ ⓐ
Inspector:	**Camden Five**
Paws & Claws Rating:	🐾 🐾 🐾 🐾 🐾

Notes:
Several flavours and sizes for all ages of feline. A recent addition is for Indoor Cats, to help hairballs, weight and litter odour. There is also a Lightweight Control variety.

Supplementary Reports:
Chicken, Duck & Rabbit Bibi 4, Boysie 5, Ninja 5
Indoor Chicken + Added Vegetables Bronte 3, Waldo 3
Kitten Chicken, Carrots & Milk Jack 5, Ninja 4
Rabbit, Turkey & Vegetables Bibi 4, Boysie 5, FB 3, Mimi 3,
  Toozie 4
Senior Chicken, Carrots & Rice Livingstone 4, Shoes 4, Sox 4,
  Toozie 4

Human Comments:
All the inspectors enjoyed this range.

Inspector's Comment:
It disappeared without trace – bones and all!

Food Report No. 24

Gourmet Classic

Flavour:	Salmon & Shrimp in a Seafood Jelly
Packaging:	
Food Type:	
Manufacturer:	Nestlé Purina Petcare
Pack Size:	100g
Available From:	P S @
Inspector:	**Bronte**
Paws & Claws Rating:	🐾 🐾 🐾

Notes:
One of the more expensive
ranges by Purina.

Supplementary Reports:
Chicken & Herbs in Jelly
Bennett Jr 4, Waldo 4; *Chicken
& Turkey in Terrine* Jack 0,
Bronte 4, Ninja 3, Sox 4;
Game & Vegetables in Terrine
Livingstone 2, Shoes 3

Inspector's Comment:
*As Oscar Wilde would say,
this was a cat food of average
importance.*

Food Report No. 25
Gourmet Gold

Flavour:	Rabbit & Game
Packaging:	🥫
Food Type:	💧
Manufacturer:	Nestlé Purina Petcare
Pack Size:	85g
Available From:	Ⓟ Ⓢ ⓐ
Inspector:	**Waldo**
Paws & Claws Rating:	🐾 🐾 🐾 🐾 🐾

Notes:
Another of Purina's 'deluxe' ranges for posh felines – but not much more than a mouthful and very expensive for a big cat like Waldo.

Supplementary Reports:
Beef Arnie 5, Bronte 2, Ninja 4, Sox 2; *Chicken & Liver in Gravy**
Bronte 5, Jack 1, Ninja 5, Waldo 3;
Lamb Bennett Jr 5, Livingstone
4, Poppy 4; *Ocean Fish* Arnie 5,
Bronte 3, Shoes 4, Sox 3; *Salmon
& Sole* Bennett Jr 4, Ninja 5,
Waldo 4

Inspector's Comment:
*The buck stopped here – it was
wonderful!*

Food Report No. 26
Gourmet Pearl

Flavour:	Mini Duck Fillets
Packaging:	
Food Type:	
Manufacturer:	Nestlé Purina Petcare
Pack Size:	85g
Available From:	P S a
Inspector:	Sox
Paws & Claws Rating:	🐾 🐾 🐾 🐾

Notes:
Purina call this 'A portion of connoisseur cat food offering the ultimate feline dining experience'. The range recently expanded with Ocean Delicacies – a good selection of fishy flavours in gravy.

Supplementary Reports:
Mini Beef Fillets Bibi 3, Boysie 4, FB 3, Shoes 4, Toozie 4, Waldo 4
Mini Chicken Fillets Bronte 3, Jack 0, Livingstone 3, Ninja 5, Poppy 4
Ocean Delicacies Cod and Shrimps in Gravy Arnie 4, Shoes 3
Ocean Delicacies Plaice and Shrimp in Gravy Bronte 5, Waldo 5
Ocean Delicacies Tuna and Shrimp in Gravy Bennett Jr 5, Livingstone 4
Premium Fillets with Beef Sauce Bennett Jr 3, Ninja 5, Waldo 4

Inspector's Comment:
Can we have it repeated on Munch of the Day?

Food Report No. 27

Gourmet Solitaire

Flavour:	Premium with Fillets of Beef in Sauce
Packaging:	🗑
Food Type:	💧
Manufacturer:	Nestlé Purina Petcare
Pack Size:	85g
Available From:	Ⓟ Ⓢ ⓐ
Inspector:	**Shoes**
Paws & Claws Rating:	🐾 🐾 🐾 🐾 🐾

Notes:
This is nouvelle cuisine for felines – small but expensive portions, excellent quality. Well received by the team.

Supplementary Reports:
Fillets of Beef in Sauce Bennett Jr 5, Ninja 5, Waldo 5
Salmon Flakes in Seafood Sauce Livingstone 3, Waldo 4
Tuna Flakes with Shrimp in Jelly Bronte 5

Inspector's Comment:
'My tastes are simple. I am easily satisfied but only by the best'
(Winston Churchill)

Food Report No. 28

Healthy Options

Flavour:	Chicken & Rice
Packaging:	
Food Type:	
Manufacturer:	Healthy Options Pet Food
Pack Size:	2.5kg
Available From:	(P) (S) (a)
Inspector:	**Camden Five**
Paws & Claws Rating:	🐾🐾

Notes:
This range is wheat and gluten free and contains no artificial
flavourings, colourings or preservatives; designed to help with
skin, fur and halitosis.

Supplementary Reports:
Chicken & Rice
Bronte 3, Ninja 2,
Waldo 3

Inspector's Comment:
*We don't do
healthy… We'd
rather have the
calories!*

☆

HiLife Complete & Crunchy

Flavour:	Fresh Salmon Recipe
Packaging:	
Food Type:	
Manufacturer:	Town & Country Petfoods
Pack Size:	375 g
Available From:	(P) (S) (a)
Inspector:	Poppy
Paws & Claws Rating:	🐾 🐾 🐾 🐾

Notes:
Several flavours in this range of complete dry foods; for hairball control and low in magnesium. Also available in 10kg breeder sacks.

Supplementary Reports:
Fresh Chicken Recipe
Boysie 5, Bronte 3, Jack 4, Ninja 3, Sox 5, Toozie 5, Waldo 4

Inspector's Comment:
My idea of a balanced diet is a biscuit in each paw!

Food Report No. 30
HiLife Perfection

Flavour:	Steamed Hake & Tuna*
Packaging:	
Food Type:	
Manufacturer:	Town & Country Petfoods
Pack Size:	80g
Available From:	Ⓟ Ⓢ ⓐ
Inspector:	**Bronte**
Paws & Claws Rating:	🐾 🐾 🐾 🐾 🐾

Notes:
A recent Super Premium range from Town & Country Petfoods,
which delighted our inspectors.

Supplementary Reports:
Poached Salmon with Seabream Bennett Jr 4, Livingstone 4,
  Waldo 5
Steamed Hake & Tuna Livingstone 5, Ninja 4, Sox 5, Waldo 5
Tender Chicken with Bacon Arnie 4, Bronte 4, Waldo 4

OUT OF THIS WORLD!

Inspector's Comment: *Absolutely out of this world!*

Food Report No. 31
HiLife Petit Pâté

Flavour:	Turkey & Giblets
Packaging:	🥫
Food Type:	💧
Manufacturer:	Town & Country Petfoods
Pack Size:	85g
Available From:	Ⓟ Ⓢ ⓐ
Inspector:	**Bennett Jr**
Paws & Claws Rating:	🐾 🐾 🐾 🐾

Notes:
Several ranges including single-serve pouches with a good variety of flavours. The Essential 85g tins have a selection of fishy and meaty ingredients. Also available are 170g and 400g sizes with different combinations. A recent find by the inspectors is Cherish.

Supplementary Reports:
Cherish Mixed Fish in Jelly Bronte 4, Waldo 3
Salmon Pâté Bibi 5, Boysie 1, Bronte 4, Mimi 5, Toozie 5
Tuna Imperial Jack 1, Shoes 4, Waldo 3
Tuna with Chicken Arnie 4, Livingstone 1, Shoes 2
Tuna with Shrimp Bennett Jr 5, Shoes 2, Waldo 4

Inspector's Comment: *This flavour is almost on another level!*

Food Report No. 32
HiLife 60% Real Meat

Flavour:	Pork & Game in Jelly
Packaging:	
Food Type:	
Manufacturer:	Town & Country Petfoods
Pack Size:	100g
Available From:	(P) (S) (a)
Inspector:	**Livingstone**
Paws & Claws Rating:	🐾 🐾 🐾

Notes:
HiLife also produce a range of foods for both kittens and the more mature feline in a good variety of flavours and sizes.

Supplementary Reports:
Diced Beef Bibi 4, Boysie 5, FB 4, Toozie 4; *Real Poultry* Bennett Jr 4, Mimi 4, Sox 4; *Sardine & Mackerel* Livingstone 1, Shoes 3, Waldo 3; *Tuna with Salmon* Arnie 5, Boysie 5, FB 4, Ninja 2, Shoes 4, Waldo 5

Inspector's Comment:
The road to a successful cat food is still under construction.

Food Report No. 33
Hill's Science Plan

Flavour:	Adult Indoor Cat – Chicken
Packaging:	
Food Type:	
Manufacturer:	Hill's Pet Nutrition
Pack Size:	300g
Available From:	P S @ V
Inspector:	**Arnie**
Paws & Claws Rating:	🐾 🐾 🐾

Notes:
A large range of complete dry and wet foods in several sizes for kittens, adults and senior felines. They also have specific foods for lifestyle and minor health problems such as Oral Care, Light, Sensitive Stomach and Hairball. Hill's have a range of Wet and Dry Prescription Diets, available only through vets and prescribed under medical supervision.

Supplementary Reports:
*Feline Adult Chicken** Arnie 4; *Feline Kitten Chicken* Jack 3; *Light Adult* Sox 1; *Oral Care* Bronte 2, Waldo 1

Human Comments:
A health-orientated range but the inspectors could take it or leave it.

Inspector's Comment: *Press F1 to pause but F2 to continue.*

Hill's Science Plan

Flavour:	Hairball Control Adult – Chicken & Turkey
Packaging:	
Food Type:	
Manufacturer:	Hill's Pet Nutrition
Pack Size:	300g
Available From:	P S @
Inspector:	**Camden Five**
Paws & Claws Rating:	🐾 🐾 🐾

Notes:
Hairball Control assists feline digestion to combat throwing up.
Also produced for seniors and in Light. Other varieties, sizes
and flavours available in this healthy
range.

Supplementary Reports:
Hairball Control Adult
Bronte 1, Waldo 2

Inspector's Comment:
The taste was average but the hairball control was good!

Food Report No. 35
Hill's Science Plan

Flavour:	Adult with Ocean Fish
Packaging:	🗑
Food Type:	💧
Manufacturer:	Hill's Pet Nutrition
Pack Size:	85g
Available From:	Ⓟ Ⓢ ⓐ
Inspector:	**Waldo**
Paws & Claws Rating:	🐾 🐾 🐾 🐾

Notes:
Available in several tin sizes and flavours, and for different feline ages.

Supplementary Reports:
Adult Beef Bennett Jr 2, Livingstone 3, Shoes 3; *Adult Light* Sox 3; *Chicken & Liver* Arnie 1, Poppy 3, Sox 3; *Feline k/d Kidney* Bronte 2 (under her doctor's supervision); *Feline i/d Intestinal* Bronte 4 (under her doctor's supervision); *Kitten Chicken* Jack 1, Toozie 4, Waldo 4; *Light Chicken* Bennett Jr 4, Sox 1

Inspector's Comment:
Definitely food for thought!

Food Report No. 36

Iams Active Mature 7+

Flavour:	Chicken
Packaging:	
Food Type:	
Manufacturer:	Iams
Pack Size:	300g
Available From:	(P) (S) (a)
Inspector:	Camden Five
Paws & Claws Rating:	🐾 🐾 🐾 🐾

Notes:
Well-thought-out complete dry-food range in various flavours and sizes; aimed at specific feline ages and problems such as weight, sensitive stomach and hairball control.

Supplementary Reports:
*Adult Lamb** Boysie 4, FB 4, Livingstone 3, Mimi 2
Kitten & Junior Chicken Jack 4, Waldo 4
Light Chicken Bibi 3, Boysie 3, FB 2, Mimi 1, Poppy 2, Toozie 2
Senior Chicken Bronte 3

Inspector's Comment:
Eat right, stay fit and enjoy your retirement…

Food Report No. 37
Iams Adult 1+

Flavour:	Lamb
Packaging:	🥫
Food Type:	💧
Manufacturer:	Iams
Pack Size:	170g
Available From:	Ⓟ Ⓢ ⓐ
Inspector:	**Poppy**
Paws & Claws Rating:	🐾 🐾 🐾 🐾

Notes:
Various flavours and sizes for the kitten, junior, adult and senior felines. A new wet range called Select Bites in Gravy is available for Kittens, Adults 1+, Active Mature 7+ and for Seniors 11+ in boxes of ten or twelve pouches.

Supplementary Reports:
Adult 1+ Chicken Arnie 2, Bronte 2, Jack 0, Livingstone 1, Mimi 2
Junior 0–1 Chicken Jack 5
Ocean Fish Bronte 3, Jack 0, Livingstone 2, Sox 3, Waldo 4
Turkey Bennett Jr 4, Bibi 4, Boysie 4, FB 3, Mimi 3, Toozie 4
Select Bites Adult 1+ Beef Arnie 3, Waldo 4
Select Bites Adult 1+ Ocean Fish Jack 5, Livingstone 4, Waldo 4
Select Bites Adult 1+ Salmon Shoes 4, Waldo 4
Select Bites Seniors 11+ Chicken Bronte 4, Ninja 3, Sox 3

Inspector's Comment: *This one deserves a bouquet!*

Food Report No. 38
James Wellbeloved

Flavour:	Adult Lamb & Rice*
Packaging:	
Food Type:	
Manufacturer:	Crown Pet Foods Ltd
Pack Size:	225g
Available From:	Ⓟ Ⓢ ⓐ
Inspector:	**Camden Five**
Paws & Claws Rating:	🐾 🐾 🐾 🐾 🐾

Notes:
With natural cranberry extract. This range is spread over Kitten, Adult, Senior and Light varieties, in several flavours and sizes; no added preservatives, flavour or colours.

Supplementary Reports:
Adult Duck & Rice Bennett Jr 2, FB 4, Mimi 3
Adult Ocean White Fish & Rice Shoes 3
Adult Turkey & Rice Livingstone 1
Kitten Duck & Rice Bibi 4, Jack 5, Ninja 2, Toozie 5
Kitten Turkey & Rice Jack 1, Waldo 2
Light Lamb & Rice Arnie 4, Ninja 5
Senior Turkey & Rice Bronte 5, Shoes 3

Inspector's Comment: *This was pawesome!*

Katkins

Flavour:	Beef & Chicken Chunks in Gravy
Packaging:	🥫
Food Type:	💧
Manufacturer:	Masterfoods
Pack Size:	400g
Available From:	Ⓟ Ⓢ ⓐ
Inspector:	**Shoes**
Paws & Claws Rating:	🐾 🐾

Notes:
Available in several flavours in jelly
or gravy.

Supplementary Reports:
Chicken & Rabbit in Jelly Shoes 2,
Waldo 1; *Rabbit & Lamb Chunks in
Gravy* Arnie 2, Bronte 2; *Salmon
Chunks in Jelly* Bennett Jr 3,
Bronte 5, Livingstone 3, Shoes 3,
Sox 3

Inspector's Comment:
*This food has delusions
of adequacy.*

Food Report No. 40
Kitekat

Flavour:	Duck & Turkey in Jelly
Packaging:	🥫
Food Type:	💧
Manufacturer:	Masterfoods
Pack Size:	400g
Available From:	Ⓟ ⑤ ⓐ
Inspector:	Sox
Paws & Claws Rating:	🐾 🐾 🐾

Notes:
The godfather of feline food now transformed by more modern recipes. Produced in a large variety of flavour combinations and sizes including single and 200g double-serve portions. A complete dry-food range is also available.

Supplementary Reports:
Chicken & Rabbit in Gravy Bronte 4, Livingstone 2, Shoes 4; *Lamb & Beef in Jelly* Bronte 5, Jack 0, Livingstone 4, Ninja 1, Waldo 4; *Rabbit in Gravy* Arnie 5, Bennett Jr 5, Poppy 3, Sox 4

Inspector's Comment:
There's no cat food like an old cat food!

Food Report No. 41

Kitekat

Flavour:	Trout
Packaging:	🗑
Food Type:	💧
Manufacturer:	Masterfoods
Pack Size:	100g
Available From:	Ⓟ Ⓢ ⓐ
Inspector:	**Arnie**
Paws & Claws Rating:	🐾 🐾 🐾 🐾

Notes:
This range of Kitekat pouches also comes in 200g portions –
useful for a two-feline family or hungry moggies.

Supplementary Reports:
Beef in Jelly Bronte 2, Sox 3, Waldo 3
Chicken in Jelly Arnie 5, Bennett Jr 3, Poppy 4
Cod in Jelly Poppy 3
Duck in Jelly Bronte 3, Jack 3, Sox 2
Lamb in Gravy Arnie 4, Bennett Jr 4, Livingstone 4, Ninja 3
Rabbit in Gravy Livingstone 5, Sox 4, Waldo 3
Tuna in Jelly Arnie 5, Bronte 5, Shoes 4

Human Comments:
Kitekat is still very much a name to respect in the world of cat food.

Inspector's Comment:
This was an out-of-windows experience…

Food Report No. 42
Marks & Spencer Gourmet

Flavour:	Goose
Packaging:	
Food Type:	
Manufacturer:	Marks & Spencer
Pack Size:	100g
Available From:	⑤ (Marks & Spencer)
Inspector:	**Bronte**
Paws & Claws Rating:	🐾 🐾 🐾 🐾 🐾

Notes:
One of several well-received ranges from the
Marks & Spencer brand.

Supplementary Reports:
Beef & Heart Bennett Jr 4, Bibi 4, Boysie 4, Mimi 3, Toozie 4,
 Waldo 4
Chicken Bronte 3, Livingstone 5, Shoes 5
Chicken & Tuna Arnie 4, Bronte 3, Sox 3, Waldo 2
Duck Boysie 4, Jack 4, Toozie 4, Waldo 4
Lamb & Chicken Arnie 5, Bronte 4, Shoes 3, Sox 4
Rabbit Jack 5, Ninja 5
Salmon & Cod Arnie 4, Bennett Jr 3, Ninja 4, Poppy 4
Turkey Bronte 3, Livingstone 5, Mimi 3, Shoes 4, Toozie 4

Inspector's Comment:
'This is a far, far better thing that I eat now'
(Charles Dickens, *1859*)

Food Report No. 43
Marks & Spencer Luxury

Flavour:	Sardine & Crab in Jelly
Packaging:	
Food Type:	
Manufacturer:	Marks & Spencer
Pack Size:	170 g
Available From:	⑤ (Marks & Spencer)
Inspector:	**Livingstone**
Paws & Claws Rating:	🐾 🐾 🐾 🐾

Notes:
Another interesting range
from Marks & Spencer with
tasty flavour combinations.

Supplementary Reports:
Mackerel & Tuna Bronte 5,
Sox 3, Waldo 5; *Sardine in
Lobster Jelly* Jack 2, Ninja 1,
Shoes 4; *Tuna in Jelly* Arnie 3,
Bennett Jr 1, Bronte 2, Sox 4

Inspector's Comment:
*Our statistics department
reports that this cat
food is closer to the top
than to the bottom.*

Food Report No. 44

Marks & Spencer Total Balance

Flavour:	Chicken
Packaging:	
Food Type:	
Manufacturer:	Marks & Spencer
Pack Size:	400g
Available From:	⑤ (Marks & Spencer)
Inspector:	**Camden Five**
Paws & Claws Rating:	🐾 🐾 🐾 🐾

Notes:
A complete dry-food range in
small re-sealable sacks.

Supplementary Report:
Chicken Shoes 4

Inspector's Comment:
*Chickens are the only creatures
you can eat before they are born
and after they are dead!*

Food Report No. 45
Miamor

Flavour:	Tuna & Calamari
Packaging:	
Food Type:	
Manufacturer:	Finnern
Pack Size:	100g
Available From:	
Inspector:	**Ninja**
Paws & Claws Rating:	

Notes:
Dolphin-friendly tuna. An overseas brand purchased online with a really interesting range of flavour combinations; not found in supermarkets or pet shops. Very expensive with delivery charges.

Supplementary Reports:
Chicken & Ham Bronte 5, Jack 3, Waldo 4
Chicken & Heart Arnie 3, Bennett Jr 5, Shoes 4
Tuna & Tuna Liver Bibi 4, Boysie 5, FB 4, Jack 5, Mimi 4,
Toozie 5
Tuna & Vegetables Livingstone 4, Sox 5

Inspector's Comment:
This cat food is like meeting God without dying!

Morrisons My Cat

Flavour:	Beef & Lamb Fine Cuts in Jelly
Packaging:	🥫
Food Type:	💧
Manufacturer:	Morrisons
Pack Size:	400g
Available From:	Ⓢ (Morrisons)
Inspector:	**Sox**
Paws & Claws Rating:	🐾 🐾 🐾

Notes:
An own-label brand with comprehensive ranges for all feline tastes and pockets: Select Cuts, Chunks in Jelly and Gravy, Gourmet, Economy and Senior. All reasonably priced. Produced in a variety of flavours and pack sizes.

Supplementary Reports:
Beef & Rabbit in Jelly Jack 3, Ninja 3, Shoes 4
Chicken & Rabbit in Jelly Ninja 2, Sox 3
Cod & Prawn in Jelly Bibi 1, Mimi 2, Sox 4, Toozie 2
Duck & Heart in Gravy Arnie 1, Shoes 4
Lamb & Chicken in Jelly Jack 0, Ninja 2
Salmon & Tuna in Jelly Boysie 2, Livingstone 3

Inspector's Comment:
As my tennis partner used to say, you cannot be serious!

Food Report No. 47

Morrisons My Cat Gourmet

Flavour:	Salmon & Ocean Fish
Packaging:	
Food Type:	
Manufacturer:	Morrisons
Pack Size:	100g
Available from:	Ⓢ (Morrisons)
Inspector:	**Bennett Jr**
Paws & Claws Rating:	🐾 🐾

Notes:
Part of a typical supermarket range, available in a variety of flavours.

Supplementary Reports:
Chicken & Game in Jelly Arnie 1, Shoes 2, Sox 1; *Turkey & Chicken* Bronte 3, Jack 3, Ninja 3

Inspector's Comment:
The most memorable feature of this food was that I ate it on a Thursday.

Food Report No. 48
Morrisons My Cat Supermeat

Flavour:	Tuna
Packaging:	🥫
Food Type:	🌢
Manufacturer:	Morrisons
Pack Size:	390g
Available from:	Ⓢ (Morrisons)
Inspector:	**Jack**
Paws & Claws Rating:	🐾 🐾 🐾

Notes:
Various traditional flavours.

Supplementary Reports:
Prawn Arnie 0, Ninja 1;
Salmon Bennett Jr 1,
Livingstone 1

Human Comments:
*A rather uninspiring
range. Most felines
like something to
chew on.*

**Inspector's
Comment:**
*Not worth coming
home for.*

Food Report No. 49
Nutro Choice Adult

Flavour:	Turkey & Duck
Packaging:	🥫
Food Type:	💧
Manufacturer:	Nutro Products
Pack Size:	85g
Available From:	@
Inspector:	**Waldo**
Paws & Claws Rating:	🐾 🐾 🐾 🐾

Notes:
An American brand found online with various ranges under
the Nutro label – Junior, Adult, Weight Management, Senior,
Gourmet and Natural Choice – in several sizes. Also available are
similar ranges of complete dry foods.

Supplementary Reports:
Adult Chicken & Liver in Gravy Bennett Jr 3, Jack 5,
    Livingstone 2, Ninja 5
Fish Arnie 1, Bronte 3, Waldo 4
Gourmet Mini Salmon & Whitefish Bronte 4, Waldo 3
Kitten Jack 3
Turkey & Duck Bennett Jr 4, Bibi 3, Boysie 4, FB 3, Livingstone 5
Weight Management Chicken & Liver in Gravy Poppy 4, Shoes 3

Inspector's Comment:
One instinctively knows when something is right.

Nutro Choice Complete

Flavour:	Adult Salmon
Packaging:	
Food Type:	
Manufacturer:	Nutro Products
Pack Size:	300g
Available From:	
Inspector:	**Sox**
Paws & Claws Rating:	🐾 🐾 🐾 🐾 🐾

Notes:

An American complete dry-food range also available for Kittens, Lactating Mothers, Seniors and Hairball Control in several flavours and sizes.

Supplementary Reports:

Adult Chicken Bennett Jr 5, Ninja 3; *Kitten* Jack 5; *Senior Chicken* Bibi 3, Boysie 4, FB 4, Mimi 3, Toozie 4

Inspector's Comment:

This was so good, it stopped me in my tracks!

SKREECH

Food Report No. 51
Olli

Flavour:	Salmon, Herring & Shrimp*
Packaging:	🗔
Food Type:	☀
Manufacturer:	Butcher's Pet Care
Pack Size:	400g
Available From:	Ⓟ Ⓢ ⓐ
Inspector:	**Ninja**
Paws & Claws Rating:	🐾 🐾 🐾 🐾

Notes:
A fairly recent range with a sensible re-sealable lid from the same stable as Classic Cat Food (Reports 11 and 12). The newest addition to the Olli range is a wet 100g cat food in a disposable dish in four interesting flavours in either sauce or gravy. Another clever packaging idea from Olli and ideal for the picnicking or travelling feline, or humans that hate washing cat-food bowls.

Supplementary Reports:
Fresh Chicken with Duck & Liver
Bennett Jr 2, Bronte 3, Waldo 4;
Salmon, Herring & Shrimp Bibi 2, Boysie 4, FB 4, Mimi 5, Shoes 3, Toozie 4

Inspector's Comment:
I really flipped my lid over this one!

Food Report No. 52
One Cat Adult

Flavour:	Chicken & Rice*
Packaging:	
Food Type:	
Manufacturer:	Nestlé Purina Petcare
Pack Size:	800g
Available From:	Ⓟ Ⓢ ⓐ
Inspector:	**Camden Five**
Paws & Claws Rating:	🐾 🐾 🐾 🐾 🐾

Notes:
Complete dry food available in several ranges for weight maintenance (Light), Kitten, Adult and Senior, with various flavours and sizes.

Supplementary Reports:
Beef & Rice Bibi 5, Boysie 5, FB 5, Mimi 5, Toozie 5
Hairball Turkey & Rice Bennett Jr 4, Mimi 4, Waldo 5
Light Chicken & Rice Boysie 4, Bronte 4, Waldo 4
Salmon & Rice Arnie 5, Livingstone 5, Sox 4, Waldo 4
Senior Chicken & Rice Bennett Jr 5, Bronte 5, Ninja 4

Inspector's Comment:
This was so good it deserved a licence to print money.

Food Report No. 53
Pascoe's Natural Complete

Flavour:	Rich in Nordic Fish & Added Vegetables
Packaging:	
Food Type:	
Manufacturer:	Pascoe's
Pack Size:	375g
Available From:	P S @
Inspector:	**Bronte**
Paws & Claws Rating:	🐾 🐾

Notes:
100% organic and non GM. Research found only one flavour and size.

Supplementary Reports:
Rich in Nordic Fish & Added Vegetables Bibi 1, Boysie 1, FB 2, Jack 0, Mimi 1, Ninja 0

Inspector's Comment:
Not even a good title could make an average cat food taste great.

Food Report No. 54
Pero Organic Petfood

Flavour:	Chicken, Rice & Vegetables
Packaging:	
Food Type:	
Manufacturer:	Pero Petfoods
Pack Size:	400g
Available From:	Ⓟ Ⓢ ⓐ
Inspector:	**Jack**
Paws & Claws Rating:	🐾 🐾

Notes:
Organic, non GM and hypo-allergenic; only natural ingredients with no artificial colours or added preservatives.

Supplementary Reports:
Chicken, Rice & Vegetables Boysie 1, FB 0, Livingstone 1, Toozie 1; *Fish & Rice* Bronte 2, Waldo 3

Inspector's Comment:
Couldn't quite cut my teeth on this…

Food Report No. 55
Pro Plan Adult

Flavour:	Duck & Rice*
Packaging:	
Food Type:	
Manufacturer:	Nestlé Purina Petcare
Pack Size:	400g
Available From:	Ⓟ Ⓢ ⓐ
Inspector:	**Camden Five**
Paws & Claws Rating:	🐾 🐾 🐾 🐾 🐾

Notes:
Another healthy Purina brand with Delicate, Kitten, Adult and
Senior ranges; various flavours and sizes.

Supplementary Reports:
Delicate Bibi 4, FB 4, Jack 3, Ninja 4, Toozie 5
Senior Chicken & Rice Bronte 5, Livingstone 4

Inspector's Comment: *This was the cat's pyjamas.*

Food Report No. 56
Royal Canin

Flavour:	Maine Coon 31
Packaging:	
Food Type:	
Manufacturer:	Royal Canin
Pack Size:	100g
Available From:	P S @
Inspector:	Waldo
Paws & Claws Rating:	🐾 🐾 🐾 🐾 🐾

Notes:
Part of a range for specific breeds with their own individual requirements; these include Siamese, Persian and Maine Coon. Royal Canin have a large range of dry foods for felines of all ages and for those with special lifestyles or medical conditions, such as Indoor Weight Management, Growth, Convalescence Support, Outdoor 30 – High Energy, Hairball, Dental, Beauty & Care and Hypo-allergenic.

Supplementary Reports:
Exigent 35/30 Bennett Jr 4, Shoes 4
Growth Digest & Dental Livingstone 4
Intense Hairball 34 Bibi 4, Boysie 4, FB 4, Mimi 4, Toozie 5
Oral Sensitive 30 Arnie 5
Senior Kidney & Osteo Bronte 3, Ninja 1
Sensible 33 Arnie 4, Bennett Jr 2, FB 4, Poppy 3, Shoes 3

Inspector's Comment:
It's tough at the top but this was made just for me!

Food Report No. 57

Sainsbury's Paws Adult

Flavour:	Lamb & Heart Chunks in Jelly
Packaging:	🗑
Food Type:	💧
Manufacturer:	Sainsbury's
Pack Size:	400g
Available From:	Ⓢ (Sainsbury's)
Inspector:	**Jack**
Paws & Claws Rating:	🐾 🐾 🐾

Notes:
An own-label brand with several ranges in different flavours and sizes; available as single-serve pouches, foils and tins.

Supplementary Reports:
Beef & Game Chunks in Gravy Bronte 3; *Lamb & Chicken* Bennett Jr 2, Waldo 2; *Salmon in Jelly* Boysie 4, FB 2, Mimi 1, Poppy 3, Toozie 3; *Salmon & Plaice Chunks in Gravy* Livingstone 3, Waldo 3; *Turkey & Ham Chunks in Jelly* Poppy 2; *Select Cuts* Chicken & Turkey in Jelly* Jack 1, Livingstone 2, Ninja 2, Waldo 3; *Salmon* Bennett Jr 3

Inspector's Comment:
I'm not sure about this…
Can I phone a friend?

Sainsbury's Paws Complete

Flavour:	Herring, Tuna & Vegetables
Packaging:	
Food Type:	
Manufacturer:	Sainsbury's
Pack Size:	375g
Available From:	⑤ (Sainsbury's)
Inspector:	Poppy
Paws & Claws Rating:	🐾 🐾

Notes:
A well-known supermarket brand in several flavours and sizes.

Supplementary Reports:
Duck, Rabbit & Vegetables Arnie 3, Sox 3; *Herring, Tuna & Vegetables* Bibi 2, Boysie 3, FB 2, Mimi 2, Toozie 2; *Salmon, Shrimp & Trout* Bronte 3, Ninja 3, Waldo 4

Inspector's Comment:
This was a few geraniums short of a full basket.

Food Report No. 59

Sainsbury's Paws for Senior Cats

Flavour:	Whitefish Chunks in Jelly
Packaging:	
Food Type:	
Manufacturer:	Sainsbury's
Pack Size:	100g
Available From:	Ⓢ (Sainsbury's)
Inspector:	**Bronte**
Paws & Claws Rating:	🐾 🐾 🐾 🐾

Notes:
Other ranges include High Society, Organic, Kitten, Adult and Senior in foils, single-serve pouches, and tins.

Supplementary Reports:
Chicken Chunks in Jelly Bennett Jr 2, Ninja 0, Waldo 2
Kitten Salmon Chunks in Jelly Jack 3, Waldo 3
Organic Chicken Chunks in Jelly Bronte 1, Jack 0, Waldo 2
Senior Lamb Original Bronte 4, Poppy 4, Waldo 3
Senior Turkey in Gravy Arnie 4, Bennett Jr 4, Livingstone 4, Shoes 4
Tuna & Turkey in Gravy Sox 3

Inspector's Comment:
*It just shows you can't judge a book
by its cover – this was an excellent read.*

Food Report No. 60
Sheba

Flavour:	Tender Goose & Garden Herbs
Packaging:	
Food Type:	
Manufacturer:	Masterfoods
Pack Size:	100g
Available From:	Ⓟ Ⓢ ⓐ
Inspector:	Sox
Paws & Claws Rating:	🐾 🐾 🐾 🐾

Notes:
Sheba ranges include Exclusive, Creation and Supreme
Selection; a large variety of interesting flavour combinations.

Supplementary Reports:
Beef & Heart in Delicate Gravy Bronte 3, Waldo 4
Chicken & Mediterranean Vegetables Bennett Jr 4, Livingstone 4
Chicken Provencale Bronte 4, Livingstone 4, Poppy 4
Delicious Morsels with Game Bronte 4, Jack 3, Ninja 5
Fine Terrine with Lamb Arnie 4, Bennett Jr 4, Shoes 4
Fricassee with Turkey & Vegetables Bronte 5, Jack 4, Waldo 4
Lamb & Spring Vegetables Livingstone 4, Shoes 4, Sox 4
Mediterranean-Style Lamb Casserole Bronte 5, Waldo 4
Salmon Arnie 2, Bennett Jr 3, Livingstone 5
Terrine of Turkey & Chicken Bibi 5, Boysie 5, FB 5, Mimi 5,
   Poppy 4, Toozie 5
Turkey & Wild Rice Bronte 5, Waldo 2

Inspector's Comment:
Game, set and almost match!

Food Report No. 61
Sheba Prime Cuts

Flavour:	Tuna & Prawns
Packaging:	🥣
Food Type:	💧
Manufacturer:	Masterfoods
Pack Size:	80g
Available From:	Ⓟ Ⓢ Ⓐ
Inspector:	Poppy
Paws & Claws Rating:	🐾 🐾 🐾 🐾 🐾

Notes:
Another range from the Sheba brand; several flavours.

Supplementary Reports:
Chicken Breast Arnie 5, Sox 2, Waldo 5
Chicken & Duck Bronte 3, Jack 4
Chicken Mousse Bennett Jr 3, Livingstone 4, Waldo 5
Tuna Bronte 5, Shoes 2, Ninja 3
Tuna & Prawns Mimi 4, Poppy 4, Shoes 4

Human Comments:
A large range of 'posh nosh' – expensive but the inspectors thought them delicious.

Inspector's Comment:
As Mae West said, 'Too much of a good thing is wonderful.'

Food Report No. 62
Somerfield Supreme Cuts

Flavour:	Chicken & Rabbit in Jelly
Packaging:	🍲
Food Type:	🌢
Manufacturer:	Somerfield
Pack Size:	100g
Available From:	Ⓢ (Somerfield)
Inspector:	**Ninja**
Paws & Claws Rating:	🐾 🐾 🐾

Notes:
This is one of several ranges from the Somerfield own-label brand; also available in single-serve pouches and tins. A good selection from one of the more reasonably priced supermarkets.

Supplementary Reports:
Chicken & Tuna Jack 3
Cod Chunks in Jelly Ninja 4, Waldo 3
Game in Jelly Bennett Jr 4, Bronte 2
Trout & Salmon in Jelly Livingstone 3, Sox 2, Waldo 3
Select Menu Chicken & Duck in Gravy Sox 3
Select Menu Salmon & Prawn Arnie 4, Shoes 4
Select Menu Tuna in Jelly Bronte 2, Livingstone 3

Inspector's Comment:
The most memorable is always the current one.
The rest just merge into a sea of foil trays.

Somerfield
Premium Chunks in Gravy

Flavour:	Beef
Packaging:	🛍
Food Type:	💧
Manufacturer:	Somerfield
Pack Size:	100g
Available From:	Ⓢ (Somerfield)
Inspector:	**Arnie**
Paws & Claws Rating:	🐾 🐾 🐾 🐾 🐾

Notes:
A good variety of flavours; 400g tins as well as single-serve pouches.

Supplementary Reports:
Beef & Lamb in Jelly Bronte 1, Sox 4, Waldo 5
Chicken & Duck in Gravy Arnie 4, Shoes 4
Duck in Gravy Bennett Jr 4, Ninja 5, Poppy 1
Lamb & Chicken in Gravy Livingstone 2, Sox 4
Salmon & Prawn in Jelly Arnie 1, Bronte 2, Waldo 5
Tuna & Salmon in Gravy Bibi 2, Boysie 1, FB 1, Mimi 2, Toozie 2

Human Comments:
A good, reasonably priced range.

Inspector's Comment:
This definitely belongs in the Favourites folder.

Food Report No. 64

Somerfield Premium Crunchies

Flavour:	Salmon, Shrimp & Tuna
Packaging:	
Food Type:	
Manufacturer:	Somerfield
Pack Size:	375g
Available From:	⑤ (Somerfield)
Inspector:	**Camden Five**
Paws & Claws Rating:	🐾 🐾 🐾

Notes:
Several flavour combinations
in this complete dry range.

Supplementary Reports:
Chicken, Turkey & Milk
Bibi 3, Boysie 3, FB 3,
Mimi 1, Toozie 2

**Inspector's
Comment:**
*When it comes to the
crunch it will be all
right on the night!*

QUIET PLEASE
REHEARSAL
IN PROGRESS

Food Report No. 65
Tesco Premium Cat Crunchies

Flavour:	Turkey, Chicken & Vegetables
Packaging:	
Food Type:	
Manufacturer:	Tesco
Pack Size:	375g
Available From:	⑤ (Tesco)
Inspector:	**Shoes**
Paws & Claws Rating:	🐾 🐾

Notes:
Several flavour combinations and sizes in
this complete dry range. Also available
is the Balance range for Kittens, Adults,
Seniors and Hairball Control.

Supplementary Reports:
Duck, Rabbit, Chicken & Vegetables
Livingstone 3, Waldo 3; *Herring,
Pilchard & Chicken* Bennett
Jr 4, Livingstone 3; *Junior
Turkey & Chicken* Jack 3

Inspector's Comment:
*Missing the sweet smell
of success.*

Food Report No. 66
Tesco Premium Cuts in Gravy

Flavour:	Duck
Packaging:	🧂
Food Type:	🌢
Manufacturer:	Tesco
Pack Size:	100g
Available From:	⑤ (Tesco)
Inspector:	**Livingstone**
Paws & Claws Rating:	🐾 🐾 🐾 🐾 🐾

Notes:
One of several ranges from Tesco's own label; range also includes Economy, Supreme Cuts, Supreme Meaty Cuts, Junior and Senior, in varying sizes and packaging.

Supplementary Reports:
Beef in Gravy Bronte 5, Jack 1, Ninja 0, Waldo 4
Chicken & Liver in Gravy Jack 1, Ninja 1
Chicken & Turkey in Gravy Bennett Jr 3, Waldo 3
Cod in Jelly Bennett Jr 5, Bibi 4, Boysie 4, FB 4, Mimi 3, Toozie 4
Rabbit & Turkey in Jelly Poppy 3, Shoes 3, Sox 3
Salmon & Prawn in Jelly Bronte 4, Jack 4, Toozie 3, Waldo 5
Trout in Jelly Jack 1, Ninja 3, Shoes 3
Tuna in Jelly Bennett Jr 5, Bibi 2, Boysie 4, FB 3, Livingstone 4

Inspector's Comment:
Delicious – definitely worth getting on the gravy train for!

Food Report No. 67
Tesco Supreme Cuts in Jelly

Flavour:	Cod & Salmon
Packaging:	
Food Type:	
Manufacturer:	Tesco
Pack Size:	100g
Available From:	Ⓢ (Tesco)
Inspector:	**Bennett Jr**
Paws & Claws Rating:	🐾 🐾 🐾 🐾

Notes:
Several flavours available in this range.

Supplementary Reports:
Chicken & Ham in Gravy Bibi 3,
Boysie 4, Ninja 1, Toozie 4, Waldo
4; *Supreme Meaty Cuts Tuna &
Trout* Bronte 3, Jack 5, Ninja 3,
Sox 1; *Supreme Meaty Cuts Turkey
& Goose* Arnie 1, Bennett Jr 3,
Livingstone 3, Shoes 1

Inspector's Comment:
*Measure for measure,
this was good eating.*

Food Report No. 68
Trophy

Flavour:	Chicken & Duck
Packaging:	
Food Type:	
Manufacturer:	Trophy Pet Foods
Pack Size:	3kg
Available From:	ⓟ ⓐ
Inspector:	**Camden Five**
Paws & Claws Rating:	🐾 🐾 🐾 🐾

Notes:
Several flavours and sizes from one of the smaller independent pet-food companies.

Supplementary Reports:
Feline Delight Bronte 3, Waldo 4; *Premium Salmon* Jack 4, Ninja 1; *Super Premium Cat* Bennett Jr 3, Livingstone 4, Shoes 4

Inspector's Comment:
Almost a winning trophy – a tasty combination.

Vitacat Healthy Balance

Flavour:	Adult 1 Year + with Chicken
Packaging:	
Food Type:	
Manufacturer:	Aldi
Pack Size:	500g
Available From:	Ⓢ (Aldi)
Inspector:	**Jack**
Paws & Claws Rating:	🐾 🐾 🐾 🐾

Notes:
A well-thought-out range and reasonably priced.
Re-sealable pack.

Supplementary Reports:
Active with Chicken FB 2, Ninja 3; *Senior 7 Years + with Chicken* Boysie 3, FB 4, Livingstone 3, Mimi 3, Toozie 4

Inspector's Comment:
This was worth taking a slow boat to China for…

Food Report No. 70
Vitacat Supreme

Flavour:	Trout & Shrimp in Jelly
Packaging:	
Food Type:	
Manufacturer:	Aldi
Pack Size:	400g
Available From:	⑤ (Aldi)
Inspector:	**Ninja**
Paws & Claws Rating:	🐾 🐾 🐾 🐾

Notes:
A large own-label brand in various ranges, flavours and sizes.

Supplementary Reports:
Beef & Lamb Chunks in Jelly
Bennett Jr 1, Bronte 3, Waldo 5;
Chicken Chunks in Jelly FB 1,
Livingstone 4, Mimi 2; *Cod
& Prawn Chunks in Jelly*
Bibi 1, Boysie 4, Livingstone 4,
Mimi 1, Toozie 3; *Duck &
Turkey Chunks in Gravy* Jack 1,
Ninja 2, Shoes 4

Inspector's Comment:
Eaten, but not forgotten!

Vitacat Supreme Cuisine Senior

Flavour:	Game & Rabbit
Packaging:	
Food Type:	
Manufacturer:	Aldi
Pack Size:	100g
Available From:	Ⓢ (Aldi)
Inspector:	**Bronte**
Paws & Claws Rating:	🐾 🐾 🐾 🐾

Notes:
Free from added colours and preservatives. Other ranges include Seasons Choice, Pâté Supreme and Supreme Cuisine Mousse, all in a variety of flavours.

Supplementary Reports:
Cuisine Junior Beef & Chicken Jack 4, Ninja 5, Waldo 4
Cuisine Mousse Salmon FB 1, Jack 4, Ninja 5
Cuisine Pâté Beef & Heart Arnie 4, Bennett Jr 4, Bronte 4, Ninja 4
Pâté & Aspic Game Bennett Jr 5, Jack 5, Ninja 4, Shoes 4, Sox 4
Seasons Choice Salmon in Seafood Sauce Jack 3, Ninja 1

Human Comments:
One of the better-received own-label brands.

AS YOU LIKE IT

Inspector's Comment: *Definitely as you like it!*

Food Report No. 72
Wafcol

Flavour:	Adult Salmon & Potato*
Packaging:	
Food Type:	
Manufacturer:	Wafcol
Pack Size:	1.5kg
Available From:	P S a
Inspector:	**Camden Five**
Paws & Claws Rating:	🐾 🐾 🐾 🐾 🐾

Notes:
A hypo-allergenic range to promote good digestion, and healthy gums and teeth; several flavours and sizes for felines of all ages.

Supplementary Report:
Kitten Salmon & Potato
Jack 4

Inspector's Comment:
Personally recommended by Mr Big.

Food Report No. 73

Waitrose Premier Recipe

Flavour:	Pheasant in Gravy
Packaging:	🥫
Food Type:	💧
Manufacturer:	Waitrose
Pack Size:	170g
Available From:	⑤ (Waitrose)
Inspector:	**Poppy**
Paws & Claws Rating:	🐾 🐾 🐾 🐾

Notes:
Another interesting range from Waitrose.

Supplementary Reports:
Chicken Dinner flavoured with Cheese Waldo 3; *Seafood Cocktail in Prawn Jelly* Arnie 4, Bennett Jr 4, Bronte 4; *Tuna with Shrimp Jelly* Livingstone 3, Shoes 3, Waldo 3

Inspector's Comment:
This should sell like hot cakes…

Waitrose Special Recipe

Flavour:	Venison & Lamb in Jelly
Packaging:	
Food Type:	
Manufacturer:	Waitrose
Pack Size:	100g
Available From:	Ⓢ (Waitrose)
Inspector:	**Shoes**
Paws & Claws Rating:	

Notes:
A relatively new selection of single-serve portions in the Waitrose Special Recipe range; several sizes and a large choice of interesting flavours. Also available: Premier, Organic and Complete Dry ranges.

Supplementary Reports:
Chicken & Turkey Sox 4, Toozie 3, Waldo 4
Duck & Lamb Arnie 4, Bronte 5, FB 3, Shoes 3
Liver & Game Chunks in Gravy Livingstone 5, Poppy 4, Sox 4
Mackerel & Coley Chunks in Jelly Arnie 4, Bennett Jr 5, Ninja 5
Plaice & Salmon in Gravy Bronte 4, Jack 4, Ninja 4
Prawn & Sole in Jelly Bennett Jr 4, Waldo 5
Rabbit & Game Bibi 3, Poppy 3, Shoes 5
Organic Terrine with Beef FB 4, Toozie 4, Waldo 4
Organic Terrine with Chicken Bennett Jr 3, Livingstone 3
Organic Terrine with Lamb Bronte 3, Ninja 3, Waldo 5

Inspector's Comment:
Never knowingly underfed!

Food Report No. 75

Waitrose Special Recipe

Flavour:	Chicken, Duck, Carrot & Cheese Filled Kibbles
Packaging:	
Food Type:	
Manufacturer:	Waitrose
Pack Size:	375g
Available From:	⑤ (Waitrose)
Inspector:	**Bennett Jr**
Paws & Claws Rating:	🐾 🐾 🐾 🐾

Notes:
One of several flavours in the Waitrose Complete Dry Food range.

Supplementary Reports:
Salmon, Trout, Carrot & Vegetables Filled Kibbles
Bennett Jr 3, Bronte 4, Jack 2, Ninja 2, Waldo 4

Inspector's Comment:
In the final analysis, sound judgement will prevail. This is definitely a four.

Waitrose Special Recipe

Flavour:	Red Mullet & Tuna Chunks in Jelly
Packaging:	🥫
Food Type:	💧
Manufacturer:	Waitrose
Pack Size:	400g
Available From:	⑤ (Waitrose)
Inspector:	**Livingstone**
Paws & Claws Rating:	🐾 🐾 🐾 🐾

Notes:
Interesting flavour combinations among the Special Recipe ranges.

Supplementary Reports:
Liver & Game Chunks in Gravy Bennett Jr 5, Jack 4, Ninja 5;
Mackerel & Coley Chunks in Jelly Arnie 4, Shoes 4, Waldo 5;
Salmon & Mackerel Chunks in Gravy Bronte 3, Poppy 3, Sox 5;
Terrine Rich in Tuna Livingstone 4, Shoes 3, Waldo 3

Human Comments:
We felt Waitrose merited an extra report because there were so many excellent flavours, almost all rated highly by the inspectors.

Inspector's Comment:
I don't mind cutting through the red tape for this one.

Whiskas Adult

Flavour:	Tuna & Vegetables
Packaging:	
Food Type:	
Manufacturer:	Masterfoods
Pack Size:	400g
Available From:	(P) (S) (a)
Inspector:	**Camden Five**
Paws & Claws Rating:	🐾 🐾 🐾 🐾

Notes:
Available for felines of all ages in other flavours and sizes.

Supplementary Reports:
Adult Chicken & Vegetables Bibi 4, Boysie 3, FB 3, Mimi 3, Toozie 3
Adult Lamb & Carrots Livingstone 4, Ninja 5, Shoes 4
Kitten Chicken & Mini Pockets with Milk Jack 2
Senior Lamb & Vegetables Bronte 3

Inspector's Comment:
This week we're on a seafood diet.
See food and eat it!

Food Report No. 78
Whiskas Junior

Flavour:	Cod
Packaging:	🫙
Food Type:	💧
Manufacturer:	Masterfoods
Pack Size:	100g
Available From:	Ⓟ ⑤ ⓐ
Inspector:	**Jack**
Paws & Claws Rating:	🐾 🐾 🐾 🐾 🐾

Notes:
A large selection of flavours in tins, foils and single- and double-serve (200g) pouches. Whiskas has specific foods for Kittens, Juniors, Adults and Seniors. Most are available in several flavour combinations, in either jelly or gravy.

Supplementary Reports:
Adult Beef in Jelly Bennett Jr 4, Livingstone 5, Waldo 5
Adult Game in Gravy Arnie 4, Bronte 1, Shoes 3
Chicken in Jelly* Arnie 3, Livingstone 4, Poppy 4, Sox 3
Duck Bibi 4, Boysie 4, Bronte 3, FB 4, Mimi 3, Ninja 5, Toozie 4
Fish FB 4, Mimi 3, Toozie 4
Junior Chicken Jack 1, Waldo 3
Junior Duck Jack 5, Ninja 4
Kitten Duck Jack 3
Lamb Casserole in Gravy Arnie 4
Senior Supermeat Chicken Bronte 2, Shoes 2
Supermeat Rabbit Bennett Jr 2, Livingstone 3

Inspector's Comment: *This went down faster than Jack's rabbit!*

Food Report No. 79
Whiskas Organic

Flavour:	Beef in Gravy
Packaging:	🗑
Food Type:	🌢
Manufacturer:	Masterfoods
Pack Size:	100g
Available From:	ⓟ ⓢ ⓐ
Inspector:	**Waldo**
Paws & Claws Rating:	🐾 🐾 🐾 🐾 🐾

Notes:
Several flavours in this organic range; generally well received by the inspectors.

Supplementary Reports:
Beef & Poultry in Gravy Bibi 3, Bronte 4, FB 4, Mimi 3, Toozie 4, Waldo 4

Poultry in Gravy Arnie 4, Jack 3, Ninja 3, Poppy 5, Shoes 3

Turkey & Vegetables in Gravy Bennett Jr 5, Bronte 5, Livingstone 3, Sox 4, Waldo 5

Inspector's Comment:
I didn't climb my way to the top of the food chain to be a vegetarian.
A rare treat.

Food Report No. 80
Yarrah Organic

Flavour:	Chicken Chunks with Salmon
Packaging:	
Food Type:	
Manufacturer:	Yarrah
Pack Size:	100g
Available From:	P S @
Inspector:	Arnie
Paws & Claws Rating:	🐾 🐾 🐾

Notes:
Several flavours and sizes in this organic range; also available as chicken-flavoured complete dry foods in 800g and 3kg sizes.

Supplementary Reports:
Chicken Chunks with Salmon
Livingstone 2, Toozie 3, Waldo 2;
Chicken Chunks with Turkey
Bennett Jr 4, Bibi 3,
Boysie 1, Bronte 1,
Mimi 3

Inspector's Comment:
This has all the right properties – but I'm not sure I'll add it to the menu!

Desserts and Treats

The choice of desserts and treats is now so extensive that we had a gastronomic predicament how best to present them. However, with our normal dedication to eating and snacking, we have sacrificed many catnapping hours to try the widest possible selection to guide the sweet-toothed feline.

Treats fall into various categories: dry chewing strips, dried fish, drops, flakes, freeze-dried, powder and even sprays for catnip (these were still classified as treats because sniffing and snorting made us very happy). Most were found to be generally good for our teeth, gums, waterworks, hairball control and general wellbeing. When reading the labels, we saw that some had added vitamins, garlic (protects against lice, ticks and vampires), parsley, eucalyptus and even cinnamon oils (good for feline aroma therapy).

Dry treats are similar to main-course biscuits – although not 'complete'. There are sprinkly ones that can be scattered over food at mealtimes in all sorts of flavours, including chicken, seafood, duck and turkey. Watch out if your human uses these – it may be yesterday's stale food back in the dish for the third time, disguised with 'tasty toppings'. Do they really think we're that silly?

Some of the hard crunchy types now have soft centres, which

make a pleasant change. Alternatively, you could try moist pellets, such as the Trout & Salmon or Chicken & Liver. We also chomped our way through some strange ones for felines, including Cranberry, Malt and Garlic – Bennett Jr says they're working on feline mouthwash. We enjoyed the real fish treats – rather messy but we still ate them at warp speed. Chewing sticks were also good. They needed to be broken into small pieces for some of the inspectors but the choice of flavours was excellent.

Milk and yoghurt drops and flakes were other options. According to Poppy, catnip (feline Class A drug) for trendy felines came in all different forms. These all rated well, leaving Jack in particular very high and excitable.

A relatively new product, which was a real winner in this section, was freeze-dried fish, chicken or prawns. They were completely natural with no additives and really hit the spot, especially for Waldo, who now has a monthly order delivered by Catflap Couriers. We quite liked them as a reward for taking pills or a bribe when visiting the vet.

The main brands sampled by the inspectors were easily found in pet shops, supermarkets and online:

Beaphar	Cat Love	Defurr-Ums
Dr Clauders	Felix	Gimpet
Good Girl	Hagen	Kookamunga
M & C	Natures:menu	Purina
Rodi	Sherleys	Thomas
Thrive	Vitakraft	Whiskas

It was decided that treats are generally quite expensive but fun to eat or nibble. So be adventurous and try them all. If you can't afford them, borrow Waldo's Catwest debit card…

Welcome to Waldo's Web

Waldo's search to find the 'ultimate' cat food led him – with the assistance of Arnie – to a plethora of interesting websites. He found that he could purchase virtually all of his requirements really easily, just by turning on the computer.

But what surprised him even more was the amazing choice available, both in the UK and overseas. All he needed was a credit card and a postcode for anything he wanted to be delivered direct to his cat flap.

The websites included food manufacturers, supermarkets, large and small pet shops, cat-activity and scratching-post sites, and personal hygiene and accessory suppliers to the 'feline about town'. Waldo, though, is still looking for computer dating for single felines.

The various sites were easy to use. As well as being a vehicle to sell feline-related products, they frequently offered useful information on dining, health, hygiene and other related topics. If you are surfing the net, look out for websites offering free samples and special offers. There are lots of them and it is a good way to experiment with new cat foods.

The following are Waldo's top five:

www.kalven.co.uk
Kalven have the most terrific range of scratching posts and cat-activity centres and will even custom-build for the rich feline that wants that 'little extra something'. Waldo bought two.

www.k9capers.com
An excellent selection of wet and dry cat foods and accessories, as well as a wide range of useful services available for the discerning feline.

www.petshop4cats.co.uk
Waldo's favourite online 'department store' with everything he could ever want.

www.purrsonaltouch.com
A great selection of feline personal hygiene equipment and other items that the indoor feline might need. They were competitive on price and efficient in delivery.

www.zooplus.co.uk
A German website that had many interesting cat foods and products that we Euroscatics had never seen or heard of before. It opened our eyes – and mouths – to being really adventurous eaters. Expensive products, but well worth trying.

Finally, although the items may appear cheaper, don't forget that postage or courier charges will be added to the purchase price when buying online. This may work out more costly than dropping in to the local supermarket – but so much more fun.

The Feline Abroad

The government has finally decided that we felines are now to be extended the right to foreign travel. As long as we have a Pet Passport, we can travel in and out of the country without ending up in jail for six months. However, according to Jack, who volunteered to be the guide's guinea pig (a difficult feat, considering he is of the feline persuasion), don't get too excited just yet. Jack's research established that before we can go anywhere there is a lot of bureaucracy to overcome prior to considering the latest travel brochures. Trains and planes come even later.

Your human will have to obtain for you all of the following:

- Microchip identification by a vet (not even Arnie can help with this).
- A certificate to confirm vaccination against rabies and necessary blood tests (with those nasty human needles).
- Required documentation as set out by DEFRA (Bennett Jr – who else? – was the ministry's feline consultant).
- A pet passport control sheet signed by a human (they don't trust us to make our own paw prints).
- Documented proof of treatment against ticks and tapeworms (more horrid pills and potions from the vet).
- A comfortable cage or carrying basket to travel in (Bennett Jr will check on the Health & Safety Regulations).

You will now see that all of the above probably cost more than a first-class ticket on Easypet Airlines.

NOTE TO ALL HUMANS

You will also need to measure the length of your feline's whiskers (in millimetres), establish eye colour, breed, distinguishing markings, and any scars or old war wounds that can also help identification.

We strongly advise that you check with DEFRA (Department for Environment, Food and Rural Affairs) and your vet to ensure that all your feline's documentation is absolutely correct. PETS Helpline: **0870 241 1710**.

Failure to comply with all the medical requirements means a statutory six months behind bars with no 'get out of jail free' cards and definitely no time off for good behaviour.

NOTE TO ALL FELINES (NOT A DEFRA REQUIREMENT)

When you're having your picture taken, make sure you remove all your jewellery (including your favourite collar) and sunglasses as they are banned. Only full frontals are permitted – no profiles are allowed, whether or not you look better from the side.

The Good Cat Food Guide Awards

The Golden Whiskers Award for
the Best Wet Cat Food

Nominees:

Classic – Game in Jelly

Felix – Duck & Heart in Jelly

Gourmet Gold – Chicken & Liver in Gravy

HiLife Perfection – Steamed Hake & Tuna

Sheba – Delicious Morsels with Chicken & Turkey

Whiskas – Chicken in Jelly

THE WINNER IS WHISKAS – CHICKEN IN JELLY

The Golden Whiskers Award for
the Best Dry Cat Food

Nominees:

Go-Cat Vitality+ – Tuna, Herring & Vegetables

Hill's Science Plan – Feline Adult Chicken

Iams Complete Adult – Lamb

Olli – Salmon, Herring & Shrimp

One Cat Adult – Chicken & Rice

Pro Plan Adult – Duck & Rice

THE WINNER IS ONE CAT ADULT – CHICKEN & RICE

The Golden Whiskers Award for the Best Supermarket Range

Nominees:

Aldi Vitacat Supreme
Asda Tiger Select Cuts
Co-op Gourmet Select Cuts
Marks & Spencer Gourmet
Morrisons My Cat Gourmet
Sainsbury's Paws Select Cuts
Somerfield Premium Chunks
Tesco Supreme Cuts
Waitrose Special Recipe

THE WINNER IS WAITROSE SPECIAL RECIPE

The Golden Whiskers Award for the Best Independent Manufacturer's Range

(Maximum 3 Ranges)

Nominees:

Arden Grange – Adult Chicken & Rice (Dry)
Burgess Supa Cat – Rabbit & Chicken (Dry)
James Wellbeloved – Adult Lamb & Rice (Dry)
Wafcol – Adult Super Premium Salmon & Potato (Dry)

THE WINNER IS BURGESS SUPA CAT – RABBIT & CHICKEN

The Golden Whiskers Award for the Best Manufacturer's Range (Multiple Ranges)

Nominees:

Felix Pouches (Nestlé Purina Petcare)
Go-Cat Vitality+ Pouches (Nestlé Purina Petcare)
HiLife Pouches (Town & Country Petfoods)
Whiskas Pouches (Masterfoods)

THE WINNER IS GO-CAT VITALITY+ POUCHES

The Golden Whiskers Special Award

THE WINNER IS OLLI

For innovative packaging

The Golden Whiskers Award for the Best UK Cat Food

ALL CATEGORIES

GO-CAT VITALITY+ POUCHES

A Last Word from Waldo

During their research, the inspectors made some interesting discoveries about cat food, its manufacture, purchase and consumption. Here are our findings:

- Cat foods labelled a particular flavour may actually contain only a small amount of the named ingredient. There don't seem to be any strict legal definitions laid down by the bureaucats at DEFRA, Trading Standards or the Food Standards Agency. The PFMA recommendations are given in the Feline Fact File – so check the labels and find out what you are buying.

- Read the weight labels (either metric or avoirdupaws) because a tin that looks like 400g may be only 390g; a 100g pouch may be smaller than it appears. Also check the weights of multipacks.

- Waldo in particular found that he had difficulty eating what his predecessor used to call 'sludge pâté'. He likes to chew his food and prefers the big chunks, which many foods don't contain. These may be fine for toothless old felines but young bloods prefer to get their canines into something really meaty.

- It is usually smell rather than taste that decides whether felines will eat a food. If they sniff the bowl and immediately go out for lunch, it's because the smell is pong shui rather than feng shui.

- The choice of cat food now available is still expanding and almost too large. Much as the inspectors recommend varied eating, they would be happier with fewer ranges within a brand and consistently good quality and flavours.

● Owners with multiple-occupancy feline households, or very large felines, felt that some of the foods available were expensive for the quantity supplied.

- Don't mix old with newly opened cat food or sprinkle it with crunchy toppings as a disguise. The smell is a dead giveaway and we all know felines are smarter than humans.

- The inspectors decided that some of the 'budget' cat foods were really yuck and refused to touch them. Budget may mean what it says on the tin, but manufacturers should improve the smell and taste for those less fortunate felines who don't own a cat bowl of their own, or those reduced to eating off the *Big Issue*.

- The team also had trouble with the new trend of printing the flavours in several foreign languages and the listed ingredients so small you need a magnifying glass. Apart from Jack, who speaks a little French, and Ninja, who can manage Siamese, none of the other inspectors knew what they were eating.

- The inspectors unanimously enjoyed trying foods not previously sampled. They discovered new untried flavours, and liked being adventurous eaters. So be on the lookout for new ranges to make dining an exciting experience.

- Don't forget the delivery charges for foods ordered off the internet. Although not always value for money, some of the expensive foods are tasty, newly available and worth trying for a special occasion.

Finally, thank you for reading the guide – we hope you and your feline will benefit from our research. Many felines still prefer human food but agree that cat food has certainly come a long way since the last guide. Our investigations continue…